THE IRISH FAMINE

Colm Tóibín and Diarmaid Ferriter

THE IRISH FAMINE

A DOCUMENTARY

THOMAS DUNNE BOOKS
ST. MARTIN'S PRESS ❧ NEW YORK

THOMAS DUNNE BOOKS.
An imprint of St. Martin's Press.

THE IRISH FAMINE. Copyright © 2001 by Colm Tóibín and Diarmaid Ferriter. All rights reserved. Printed in the United States of America. No part of this book may be used or reproduced in any manner whatsoever without written permission except in the case of brief quotations embodied in critical articles or reviews. For information, address St. Martin's Press, 175 Fifth Avenue, New York, N.Y. 10010.

All illustrations copyright © *Illustrated London News*

www.stmartins.com

ISBN 0-312-30051-4

Part I previously published in part in 1998 by *London Review of Books*
Part I first published in book form titled *The Irish Famine* by Profile Books, 1999

First U.S. Edition: July 2002

10 9 8 7 6 5 4 3 2 1

Contents

**IRELAND
in the 1840s**

LONDONDERRY

DONEGAL

ANTRIM

TYRONE

Belfast

DOWN

FERMANAGH

ARMAGH

LEITRIM

MONAGHAN

SLIGO

CAVAN

LOUTH

MAYO

ROSCOMMON

Strokestown

LONGFORD

MEATH

WEST-
MEATH

DUBLIN

GALWAY

Galway

Dublin

KINGS Co

KILDARE

QUEENS Co

WICKLOW

CLARE

CARLOW

Limerick

TIPPERARY

KILKENNY

Enniscorthy

LIMERICK

WEXFORD

KERRY

WATERFORD

CORK

Cork

THE IRISH FAMINE

Colm Tóibín

The house at Coole has gone now; razed to the ground. 'They came like swallows and like swallows went,' Yeats said in 'Coole Park, 1929', imagining a time

> When all those rooms and passages are gone,
> When nettles wave upon a shapeless mound
> And saplings root among the broken stone.

Nothing now roots among the broken stone: the site where the house once stood is cemented over, as though to contain uneasy spirits in the foundations. It is a palpable absence, a warning that this is what can happen to great houses with ambiguous legacies.

The copper beech tree on which Lady Gregory's guests carved their names is close by. You can just make out some of the initials: GBS, SOC, WBY, JBY, AE. 'All That comes of the best knit to the best,' Yeats wrote in 'Upon a House Shaken by Land Agitation'. Lady Gregory, Yeats's friend and collaborator, remains a heroic presence in Irish writing at the turn of the century: dedicated, serious-minded, stalwart, practical. The house where Yeats took the master bedroom and wrote each summer would have remained a shrine to her generosity and his genius; its demolition in 1941 was a disgrace.

Augusta Persse was born in 1852, and in 1880 she married Sir William Gregory, who was thirty-five years older than her. He died in 1892, and she outlived him by forty years. Lady Gregory made herself useful to Yeats, as Roy Foster shows in his biography of the poet, because of her interest in folklore and her knowledge of the area around Coole and its people. 'John Synge, I and Augusta Gregory, thought/All that we did, all that we said or sang/Must come from contact with the soil.' Much of Yeats's work on Irish folklore was, as Foster points out, a collaboration with Lady Gregory.

Lady Gregory also wrote plays, which had to do in various ways with 'the soil'. The Coole Park she came to after her marriage in 1880 must have been haunted by the Great Famine, which began with the failure of the potato crop in certain parts of Ireland in 1845. It is recorded, for example, that on 5 April 1847 4,000 destitute labourers gathered at Gort, the nearest town to Coole Park, looking for work. In 1848 a Poor Law inspector visiting the workhouse in Gort wrote that he could scarcely 'conceive a house in a worse state, or in greater disorder'. A quarter of the population of the area sought relief in those years and many died in the most appalling circumstances. Sir William Gregory witnessed much of this and was, according to his biographer, deeply affected: 'He never forgot either the taut skin over skeletal features or the hollow voices of those wasting away from hunger and disease, nor the sight of "poor wretches" who had built "wigwams of fir branches" against his demesne wall.'

Yet in 1847, as the Famine in Ireland became increasingly serious, Sir William Gregory drafted what is often described as 'the infamous Gregory clause' in the Poor Law legislation for Ireland going through the House of Commons: any family holding more than a quarter of an acre could not be granted relief, either in or out of the workhouse, until they gave up their land.

Thus landlords who wanted to move from tillage to livestock or dairy farming would now have a valuable opportunity to do so. They would also rid themselves of bad tenants. The Gregory clause was 'a charter for land clearance and consolidation', according to Peter Gray. 'The substantial rise in evictions after 1847 was attributed largely to its introduction,' according to Christine Kinealy. For the tenants whose potato crop had failed and whose families were starving, the Gregory clause was a nightmare. As a rule, not even children were allowed to enter the workhouse until a family's land was surrendered. People had to decide: if we want to eat, we have to give up our land.

The Gregory legacy is two-sided, then: imagining Ireland (her); causing hardship and misery in Ireland that were almost unimaginable (him). In *Heathcliff and the Great Hunger* Terry Eagleton has wry words to say about the relationship between Anglo-Irish landlords and Anglo-Irish writers:

Yet it could not pass entirely unnoticed that if the forefathers of the colonial class in Ireland had been a little less intent on undermining the native culture, their emancipated sons and daughters would have needed to busy themselves rather less with restoring it. Before Lady Gregory came to collect Gaelic folk tales, her future husband William had framed the infamous Gregory clause in the depths of Famine.

In a lecture delivered on Irish radio in 1995 and published in *The Great Irish Famine: The Thomas Davis Lecture Series*, James Donnelly remarked that throughout the rest of the Famine years, the Gregory clause or 'Gregoryism' became a byword for the worst miseries of the disaster – eviction, exile, disease and death. When in 1874 Canon John O'Rourke, the parish priest of Maynooth, came to publish his *History of the Great Famine of 1847*, he declared of the Gregory clause: 'A more complete engine for the slaughter and expatriation of a people was never designed.' In case anyone might be inclined to forgive or forget (perhaps already there were a few revisionists about), O'Rourke insisted that 'Mr Gregory's words – the words of ... a pretended friend of the people – and Mr Gregory's clause are things that should be for ever remembered by the descendants of the slaughtered and expatriated small farmers of Ireland.'

Irish historians, on the whole, do not become emotional about the Famine. Like historians elsewhere, they are happier to describe and analyse than blame or use emotional language or emotional quotations. They are not in the business of writing about forgiving or forgetting: they are aware, perhaps, that we have had to listen to this sort of language for a long time in Ireland, and none of it has done us much good. But then, as I discovered from the notes on contributors in *The Great Irish Famine*, James Donnelly is a professor of history at the University of Wisconsin-Madison. He is an American of Irish extraction.

Once I knew this, I felt I understood the tone of the paragraph. Why could an Irish historian not have written it? Equally, why had I immediately and automatically disapproved of the tone? Why should we remain cool and dispassionate and oddly distant from the events of 150 years ago?

They have redecorated Pugin's Catholic cathedral in Enniscorthy, County Wexford, in the south-east of Ireland, where I grew up. I had always remembered the stone on the inside as colourless and austere, and I had liked the dullness of it. But now it is all colour; that is the way it was, we are assured, when it was built. It was by far the largest building in the town – it still is – and was built on the site of the old thatched cathedral. It must have carried the great weight of power and newness which factories had in more industrial landscapes. It was where people first learned to remain quiet in large groups, and where they learned about being on time. Until the recent restoration I had never imagined the colour: people must have been shocked by the richness of it when the doors of the cathedral opened in 1846.

The souvenir brochure which the Catholic Church in the town produced for the centenary of the cathedral in 1946 has some wonderful descriptions of the new building: 'The chancel screen of richly-carved Caen-stone runs up to the capitals of the tall granite pillars supporting the arches which separate the sanctuary from the aisles. The carved screen work is gracefully supported by a series of polished pillars of native marble which rise from plinths of Caen-stone.' Or: 'The floor of the chancel is set with encaustic tiles with designs in red, brown, pale green, white and rich Wedgwood blue.' Mass was said in this sumptuous building in 1846 and work continued on the cathedral for the next few years.

It seems incongruous now, barely possible that this wealth of detail was being incorporated into an Irish Catholic institution in 1846 and 1847, the years we associate with the Famine. The centenary brochure contains an analysis of the subscriptions made to the building fund in the 1840s. 'At the time when these were made,' the article says, 'the great Famine was sweeping through the land. Many of those whose small subscriptions helped to build Enniscorthy Cathedral must soon have known bitter hunger, starvation and death.' It goes on to list the subscribers and identify those who still had relatives in the town in 1946. I knew some of these people: Dan Bolger, for example, whose grandfather, Paul, had donated money in 1846. Dan Bolger had a shop in the town. It was hard to think of him, or any of these people, having grandparents who knew 'bitter hunger, starvation and death'. Most of them had inherited property and exuded a certain prosperity.

The story of the cathedral and those who subscribed to it makes clear to us that Catholic society in Ireland in the 1840s was graded and complex, that to suggest that it was merely England or Irish landlords who stood by while Ireland starved is to miss the point. An entire class of Irish Catholics survived the Famine; many, indeed, improved their prospects as a result of it, and this legacy may be more difficult for us to deal with in Ireland now than the legacy of those who died or emigrated.

The trustees of Lord Portsmouth are mentioned in the centenary brochure as subscribing to the cathedral fund. The following sentence is added: 'Later, in the famine years, this family, which practically owned Enniscorthy, did nothing to aid their people.' In my father's account of the Famine – he was a local historian – in the same brochure, he wrote about the rise in the price of food: the workhouse could buy oatmeal for two pounds a ton in October 1845; within a few months that had gone up to five pounds and by the end of 1846 it was twenty. He does not comment on this: there were things you could not say in 1946 about the Famine, such as that ordinary Catholic traders in the town and the stronger farmers speculated in food and made profits. Instead, he wrote:

nothing in our history, perhaps, fills us with so much pity and sorrow; pity for the poor of our country, for it was they who suffered most; no other events leave us with so much to ... wonder at – how, for instance, an ignoble ascendancy stood idly by and watched the export of great quantities of corn, exported to pay rents to absentee landlords, corn which might have saved a million lives.

It is plain from much writing about the Famine that two things happened in its aftermath. One, people blamed the English and the Ascendancy. Two, there began a great silence about class division in Catholic Ireland. It became increasingly important, as nationalist fervour grew in the years after the Famine, that Catholic Ireland, or simply 'Ireland' (the Catholic part went without saying), was presented as a nation, one and indivisible. The Famine, then, had to be blamed on the Great Other, the enemy across the water, and the victims of the Famine had to be this entire Irish nation, rather than a vulnerable section of the population.

And it became a truth universally acknowledged that this was an event we still had to come to terms with; that scholars needed to do a great deal of work before we could finally understand what happened in Ireland in the latter part of the 1840s, why it happened, and who was to blame. The first hundred issues of *Irish Historical Studies* contained only five articles on the Famine. Between the years 1974 and 1987 *Irish Economic and Social History* did not publish a single article on it. Thus we find the following remarks in Cormac O'Gráda's *Ireland: A New Economic History 1780–1939*: 'The truth about the connection between relief, wages and work effort during the Famine must have been complex, but has not been studied.' Or: 'The deals that farmers made with those they retained have not been studied in the Irish context.' Or: 'The food content of the diet' offered in the soup kitchens 'still awaits definitive analysis.' Or: 'The most obvious question about Irish famine relief – how many lives were saved by actual outlays and how much more it would have cost to save more of the lives lost – are probably unanswerable ... Perhaps detailed local study and comparative insights will answer such questions.' Or: 'A salutary feature of Sen's approach is its focus on class and distributional considerations, too long taboo in Irish historiography. It invites Irish historians to look more deeply into the part played by farmers, shopkeepers and townspeople – or, more generally, the middle classes – in preventing or exacerbating mortality.' Or: 'Many of the guardians presiding over the stingiest Poor Law Unions were middle-class Repealers' – generally Catholics in favour of repealing the 1801 Act of Union – 'not Protestant landlords. Again, few Irish Members opposed the passage of the Gregory clause in Westminster. There is ample scope for further research here by cultural, social and local historians.'

Ample indeed. In the early 1940s Eamon de Valera, who had been brought up in County Clare, a part of Ireland deeply affected by the Famine, realised that there was a need for a definitive single volume on the Famine by serious historians, and, as Taoiseach, he decided to make public money available for this. The project was taken on by Robert Dudley Edwards from University College Dublin, who promised that a book, 1,000 pages long, made up of essays by various experts, would be in print by 1946. The government released a grant of £1500. Over the next few years Edwards worked with a number of co-editors. Many setbacks befell the project and, often enough, the editors were to blame. The chapter on the medical history of the Famine had to appear without footnotes because one of the editors lost them, 'allegedly in a London taxi-cab'.

In 1950, the government was still asking for information on the project. In the early 1950s the title changed from The History of the Great Irish Famine to The Great Irish Famine:Studies in Irish History 1845–52. It finally appeared in 1956, with 436 pages of text. It was the first serious work about the Famine by modern historians, and it tells us a great deal both about the Famine and about the historians. In his essay on the saga of this book, which is included in Interpreting Irish History: The Debate on Historical Revisionism, O'Gráda writes: 'it reads more like an administrative history of the period, with the core chapters dwelling on the tragedy mainly from the standpoint of the politician, the Poor Law administrator, those who controlled passenger movements, and the medical practitioner ... Few of the contributors relied on the wealth of manuscript sources available even then on the famine years.'

De Valera was out of office by the time the book was published. 'Later,' O'Gráda writes, 'he expressed unhappiness with the book, presumably because it seemed to downplay those aspects of the tragedy that had been etched in his own memory.' O'Gráda goes on: 'Almost three decades later, that "definitive history" remains to be written, though a great deal of work has been done in the interim.'

Laziness on the part of the contributors, perhaps, a rather active social life, busy teaching schedules and problems with source material may all help to explain why the book commissioned by the government (and reissued by Lilliput Press in 1994) was half the length promised and extremely tentative in tone. In the early 1970s in University College Dublin, I studied with a few of the people involved in the project. It was clear from their bearing, the timbre of their voices and their general interest in source material that their time in British universities had been very important for them, that they were happier reading *Hansard* than going through lists of the names of people who died on coffin ships. It was equally clear that they would never have edited a book about the Famine had they not been commissioned to do so. If they did not come from a class which was largely spared the Famine and land clearance, then they certainly aspired to it.

But the problem may be endemic – wider, certainly, than the personalities and backgrounds of a few academics. It may lie in the relationship between catastrophe and analytic narrative. How do you write about the Famine? What tone do you use? It is now agreed (at least more or less) that around a million people died of disease, hunger and fever in the years between 1846 and 1849. The west of Ireland suffered most and there are people there today who claim to be haunted still by the silences and absences and emptiness that the Famine left. The political legacy was also important. It emerges most clearly in the Irish nationalist John Mitchel's *Jail Journal*, first published in New York in 1854. The Famine, he claimed, was genocide: it could have been prevented by the British. 'In every one of those years, '46, '47, '48, Ireland was exporting to England food to the value of £15 million, and had on her own soil at each harvest, good and ample provision for double her own population, notwithstanding the potato blight.' This claim persisted, as did the call that we should neither forgive nor forget. In fact, food imports for the years 1846 to 1850 exceeded exports by a ratio of two to one.

Such claims and calls make historians cringe, especially those who have spent a good part of their youth and early middle age poring over statistics in order to make a number of qualified assertions with a degree of confidence. The question of tone in Irish historical writing has been raised by Brendan Bradshaw in 'Nationalism and Historical Scholarship', an essay published in *Interpreting Irish History*. Bradshaw is concerned to show that 'value-free' history cannot work in a society such as Ireland, 'seared ... by successive waves of conquest and colonisation, by bloody wars and uprisings, by traumatic social dislocation, by lethal racial antagonisms, and, indeed, by its own 19th-century version of a holocaust'. He writes about the 'sheer neglect' of the Famine by historians, with the exception of the Government-sponsored book. He goes on:

And when eventually a second brief study appeared, thirty years after the first, yet another strategy was deployed to distance the author and her readers from the stark reality. This was by assuming an austerely clinical tone, as befitting academic discourse, and by resort to sociological euphemism and cliometric excursi, thus cerebralising and, thereby, desensitising the trauma. In short, confronted by the catastrophic dimension of Irish history, the discomfiture of the modern school of value-free historians is apparent. So is the source of their discomfiture: a conception of professionalism which denies the historian recourse to value judgements and, therefore, access to the moral and emotional register necessary to respond to human tragedy.

Surely if we want moral and emotional registers as badly as Bradshaw suggests we do, we will not look to historians: we will read novels and poems, listen to ballads, stick close to our grandmothers and say our prayers. The questions we want answered remain the same: What caused the Famine? How could it have been prevented? How many died and who were they? What was the result? The sifting of facts, the careful analysis of statistics, the painstaking study of details, the weighing up of material are what is required. We have enough moral and emotional registers (at least in Ireland we do; Bradshaw teaches at Cambridge). We need information.

That 'second brief study' which Bradshaw castigates is Mary Daly's *The*

Famine in Ireland, first published in 1986. This is a briskly written, useful book, short on emotion, long on detail and cautious examination. Daly is careful not to blame the Administration. 'The major distortion which the potato failure brought to the Irish rural economy had neither been foreseen, nor could it have been readily prevented,' she writes. She makes no attempt to pull our heartstrings. In a section on emigration, for instance, she writes: 'No account of famine emigration would be complete without a reference to coffin ships. The death rate on some ships was more than 50 per cent.' This may be an 'austerely clinical tone', but it hardly amounts to 'sociological euphemism', not to speak of 'cliometric excursi'. It allows the reader to fill in the emotion. Afterwards, Daly goes on to provide a good deal of information about death rates at sea and types of ship.

Towards the end of the book, however, her method entirely fails her, so that you can see Bradshaw's point when, after his attack on Daly, he calls on Irish historians to show 'empathy' and 'imagination'. Daly writes: 'The most potent impact, that on the famine victims, is the most impossible to assess.' (No, it isn't impossible: it is clear. The most potent impact was death.) 'The personal consequences of the disaster, however, still escape us,' she goes on. 'For survivors, it must have meant the loss of kin – people widowed, orphaned, parents who had lost most, perhaps all of their children.' There is a banality in the writing here, an insistence on sticking to a methodology that precludes any unqualified assertion and makes the prose almost comically flat.

The population of Ireland increased rapidly from the early seventeenth century. In 1600 it was just over a million: by 1841 it had risen to something over eight million. By that time half a million Irish farms were smaller than fifteen acres and almost 200,000 holdings were smaller than five acres. The west of the country, where there was less arable land, was the most densely populated. (Mayo in the west had 475 people to the square mile: Kildare, near Dublin, 187.) As the British administration saw it, these small holdings were neither practical nor sustainable. In 1848, Lord Palmerston wrote to Lord John Russell: 'It is useless to disguise the truth that any great improvement in the social system of Ireland must be founded upon an extensive change in the present state of agrarian occupation, and that this change necessarily implies a long, continued and systematic ejectment of small holders and squatting cottiers.'

One third of all agricultural land in 1845, the first year of the blight, was used for growing potatoes, which were, as we know, the staple for at least half the population. (It is estimated that some people ate seventy potatoes a day; O'Gráda puts the figure at between twelve and fourteen pounds a day.) The blight was first noticed in the autumn of 1845 in Ireland and elsewhere. The Netherlands, according to Daly, lost two thirds of its potatoes, Belgium seven eighths. In Ireland, the loss was something between one third and a half.

Sir Robert Peel, Prime Minister at the start of the blight, was well informed about conditions in Ireland. When his name is mentioned in the history books, it is normally appended to the quotation from the *Freeman's Journal* to the effect that 'no man died of famine during his Administration'. His government spent a large sum of money importing Indian corn for secret storage in Ireland and by the time it fell in the summer of 1846, private and government imports of food had filled the gap left by the blight.

It was after the election of Lord John Russell and the Whigs that the real problems began. Prices started to rise. 'Indian meal prices remained virtually stable at 1–1.2 pence per pound until the autumn of 1846,' Daly writes. 'Wheat prices averaged 47 shillings per hundredweight on the market in August 1846 but reached 70 shillings by January 1847 and 100 shillings by the following May.' And when the blight returned, it was more widespread and more severe.

What is notable about this period is the virulence of the comments about Ireland and Irish people, both landlords and peasants, made by politicians and journalists in Britain, including figures like Engels, who wrote: 'Filth and drunkenness, too, they have brought with them ... The Irishman loves his pig as the Arab loves his horse, with the difference that he sells it when it is fat enough to kill. Otherwise, he eats and sleeps with it, his children play with it, ride upon it, roll in the dirt with it.' Or Carlyle: 'The wild Milesian features, looking false ingenuity, restlessness, unreason, misery and mockery, salute you on the highways and byways. He is the sorest evil this country has to strive with.' Or Elizabeth Smith, the Scottish-born wife of a Wicklow landlord: 'The Irish landlord is in no essential different from the Irish peasant – his superior position has raised him in many points above his labouring countryman but the character of this race is common to all. The same carelessness or recklessness, call it what you will – the same indolence, the same love of pleasure, the same undue appreciation of self.' Or Lord John Russell to Lord Lansdowne in October 1846: 'The common delusion that government can convert a period of scarcity into a period of abundance is one of the most mischievous that can be entertained. But alas! the Irish have been taught many bad lessons and few good ones.' In March 1847, *The Times* declared the Irish 'a people born and bred from time immemorial, in inveterate indolence, improvidence, disorder and consequent destitution ... The astounding apathy of the Irish themselves to the most horrible scenes under their eyes and capable of relief by the smallest exertion is something absolutely without a parallel in the history of civilised nations.' In August 1847 Lord Clarendon wrote to Lord John Russell: 'We shall be equally blamed for keeping [the Irish] alive or letting them die and we have only to select between the censure of the Economists or the Philanthropists – which do you prefer?'

These are just a few examples of the dismissive tones used about Ireland at the time. If you also take into account the fact that the British government and Irish landlords wanted land clearance on a vast scale, then the obvious question arises: could it be that, on the one hand, there were these attitudes and ambitions and, on the other, there was a famine, but that the two are not necessarily connected, or not connected enough to constitute cause and effect? The Famine was caused, after all, by a potato blight and the system of land-holding meant that many people had no money to buy food. It is like an Agatha Christie novel in which everything – motive, attitude – points to an obvious suspect, but the culprit turns out to have been the vicar's wife, whom no one suspected.

In fact, nobody is suggesting that the administration actually caused the Famine. The suggestion is rather that, impelled by their contempt for Ireland and their interest in land reform, the administration caused many people to die. This is the possibility some historians are afraid to approach and others, who come to wildly different conclusions, are only too ready to entertain.

For any historian writing about Ireland in 1847 there is another problem: the copious documentary evidence about public policy and the administration of relief (or, indeed, its withholding) generated by those in charge, and the paucity of personal material about those who suffered. You can read page after page about the Famine and never come across the name of anyone who died or anything about them. In *The Famine Decade: Contemporary Accounts 1841–51*, you find the following, dated 19 April 1848:

The Rev. Mr Henry P.P. Bunenadden, county Sligo, in a memorial to the Lord Lieutenant, complained that the following persons met their deaths by hunger, owing to the neglect of the Guardians of the Boyle Union: KILSHALVEY ELECTORAL DIVISION – Mrs Kilkenny and child, after several applications for relief in vain; Mary Connell, found dead by a rick of turf; Philip M'Gowan's wife and daughter; Bryan Flanagan, found dead by the road side; Widow Davy's daughter; Andrew Davy. KILTURRA ELECTORAL DIVISION – John May and son; Pat Marren, Widow Corlely, John O'Hara, John Healy's two daughters.

What interests me here is the resonance of the names, all common in Ireland now. John Healy's two daughters, or Mary Connell, found dead by a rick of turf: the names are enough to allow you to imagine them, to think you may have known them. Pondering the names makes you wonder about the whole enterprise of historical writing itself, how little it tells us, how brittle are the analyses of administrative systems in the face of what we can imagine for ourselves just by seeing a name with a fact beside it.

It is useful to keep all this in mind when we try to understand the complex machinations of the administration in 1847 as the starving moved into the workhouse and a system of public works began. The guidelines laid down for this system were that 'it should be as repulsive as possible consistent with humanity, that is, that paupers would rather do the work than "starve".' At the end of September 1846, 26,000 men were employed on relief work: by March 1847 it was 714,000 (with 12,000 Civil Service monitors). The money they earned did not prevent those who were working from dying. 'Their bodily strength gone and spirits depressed, they have not the power to exert themselves sufficiently to earn the ordinary day's wages,' the chairman of the Board of Works wrote. The winter of 1846–47 was exceptionally cold, and a great majority of Irish labourers and potato farmers did not normally work much in the winter months, and no one owned heavy clothes. (Since there was nothing to do in winter on small holdings in the years before the Famine – the potato was growing of its own accord – it is suggested that most of them sat around the fire talking in Irish and laughing, much to the consternation of the Victorian visitor.) Instead of keeping them alive, the winter work killed them.

And the numbers – one third of the able-bodied male population – availing themselves of the public works scheme disrupted other areas of economic activity. 'No section of the economy – wages, food prices, the structure of agricultural production – remained untouched,' Daly writes. In January 1847 the administration decided to abandon public works and, encouraged by the measured success of the Quaker soup kitchens, decided to introduce outdoor relief – soup kitchens – to be organised by local committees. From mid-March people were being dismissed from public works, but the new provision was not fully operational until the late spring or, in some cases, the early summer. 'This hiatus in famine relief in the early months of 1847,' Daly writes, 'during one of the most difficult periods of all, and one marked by extremely high death-rates, is probably one of the most serious inadequacies in the whole government relief programme.' The gap is all the more difficult to understand in view of the national fast in aid of the victims of the Irish Famine in England on 24 March 1847. Supported by the Queen, it raised almost half a million pounds and helped to make people aware of what was happening in Ireland, while doing nothing to weaken their belief that the Famine was caused by Providence, as Peter Gray makes clear in *Famine, Land and Politics*.

Because the actual administration of relief was local and because the level of distress, disease and starvation varied from locality to locality, it is impossible to make many sweeping statements about the measures taken in 1847. In *Modern Ireland 1600–1972* Roy Foster examines the case of Killaloe in County Clare, where there were no deaths from starvation during the Famine, partly because of relief schemes, but mainly because of the efforts of the relief committees and the Quakers. Foster cites Sean Kierse's 1984 study of Killaloe and O'Gráda in turn calls into question the conclusions Foster reaches on the basis of 113 deaths in the fever hospital. Elsewhere, when more local studies have been done, they will complicate matters still further. The details accumulate, according to O'Gráda, 'like blobs of paint in an Impressionist painting: one needs more blobs and one needs to stand back before one can really appreciate what is going on'.

On a national scale, however, the figures retain their photo-realist quality. By August 1847 three million people were being fed every day by the state. The money was advanced by the government, to be repaid in full from the local rates. The government in London was determined that famine relief would be paid for on this basis but, especially in the west of Ireland, local levies became almost academic; even landlords were unable to pay them. With weak and starving people gathered together in such numbers, infectious diseases spread rapidly. 'The overwhelming majority of famine deaths,' Daly points out, 'occurred from typhus, relapsing fever and dysentery.'

The potato crop failed again in 1848, this time mainly in the west and the north-east. In London, in an early instance of effective spin-doctoring, there was a move to insist that the Famine was over, and that any remaining problems could be handled locally. 'What shocks,' O'Gráda writes in *The Great Irish Famine*, 'is the size of the excess mortality in 1848–50. The continuing winter mortality-peaks point like accusing fingers at the official determination to declare the crisis over in the summer of 1847.' O'Gráda has analysed the papers of Charles Trevelyan, Assistant Secretary to the Treasury, and suggests that, throughout these years, Trevelyan believed that the 'Famine had been ordained by God to teach the Irish a lesson, and therefore should not be too much interfered with'. As early as 1848, Trevelyan could refer to 'the great Irish famine of 1847' and then go on:

Unless we are much deceived, posterity will trace up to that famine the commencement of a salutary revolution in the habits of a nation long singularly unfortunate, and will acknowledge that on this, as on many other occasions, Supreme Wisdom has educed permanent good out of transient evil.

He meant, of course, that land had been cleared. These are the figures of ownership:

	1845	1851
1–5 acres	181,950	88,083
5–15 acres	311,133	191,854
15 plus	276,618	90, 401

The economist Amartya Sen has stated that 'in no other famine in the world was the proportion of people killed as large as in the Irish famines in the 1840s'. It is useful in this connection to look at the number of evictions that took place.

'It is impossible to be certain how many people were evicted during the years of the Famine and its immediate aftermath,' James Donnelly writes. 'The police began to keep an official tally only in 1849, and they recorded a total of nearly 250,000 persons as formally and permanently evicted from their holdings between 1849 and 1854.' Like Peter Gray, he also notes that Russell was opposed to evictions on this scale, but that members of his Cabinet, who had interests in Ireland, prevented legislation offering tenants greater rights. No one doubted that an eviction order was close to a death sentence, especially in the second half of the 1840s. In Kilrush, County Clare, in 18 months between 1847 and 1848, the population was reduced from 82,000 to 60,000. The *Limerick Chronicle* reported a year later:

Of those who survive, masses are plainly marked for the grave. Of the thirty-two thousand people on the relief lists of Kilrush union I shall be astonished if one half live to see another summer ... Again, in the divisions of Moyarta and Breaghford one third of the population have altogether disappeared, few or none by emigration, the great majority by eviction and the ever-miserable and mortal consequences that follow.

W. E. Vaughan, in *Landlords and Tenants in Mid-Victorian Ireland*, states that 70,000 families were evicted in the entire period 1846–54. Roy Foster suggests that the figure for evictions between 1847 and 1854 is 50,000. For all historians of the period, however, accurately calculating the number of evictions in the years before 1849 is impossible and the years afterwards extremely difficult. Roy Foster has written: 'Statistics were always problematic, raising difficulties of definition as well as occurrence.' Mary Daly suggests that 3,500 families were evicted in 1846, 6,000 in 1847 and 9,500 in 1848. 'Both pre-famine and post-famine eviction levels appear to have been relatively low,' she writes. She tells us that eviction was never part of government policy. Her insistence on playing down the importance of evictions, and refusing to blame landlords or government, is only plausible if her figures are accurate.

In 1998, Tim O'Neill, a colleague of Mary Daly's at University College Dublin, gave a lecture to a conference on Famine Culture and Politics, which was published in the volume *Famine, Land and Culture in Ireland*, edited by Carla King, in summer 2000. This densely written and closely argued lecture, entitled 'Famine Evictions', changes our entire view of the subject. O'Neill claims that 'the role of eviction in the creation of the catastrophe of the Great Famine is central ... The underestimation of eviction rates and even threats of eviction has led to a distortion of famine studies by a generation of historians.' He points out that historians have assessed statistics for evictions on the number of 'originating processes entered, rather than served'. And he insists that his colleagues have been immensely conservative in their estimation of how many holdings could be covered by a single process. 'It is clear that a single *habere* [eviction order] could lead to many evictions.' He points out, for example that, 'The sub-sheriff in Kerry recorded that he evicted 715 heads of families on foot of 39 *habere* decrees from 20 March 1847 to 10 February 1848.'

O'Neill writes that his own method of reading the returns is 'fraught with difficulties and the returns are not always consistent, but it produces a figure for Famine evictions of 97,248 heads of household or families, or approximately 486,240 persons, in the years 1846 to 1848. When the police returns are added to this for 1849 to 1854 the combined returns give a total for the period 1846 to 1854 of 144,759 families or 723,795 persons who had decrees of *habere* against them and who were evicted or threatened with eviction.' Since not all those who received writs were actually living on the holding in question, O'Neill later reduces his estimate to 579,036.

O'Neill's argument is difficult to paraphrase because it contains a detailed analysis of the niceties of land-holding and eviction processes. He is certainly convincing that one eviction order could cover more than one family; but he is less convincing about whether we should use eviction orders rather than evidence of actual evictions carried out as the basis for arriving at a figure.

'Evictions are well on the way to being written out of the history of nineteenth-century Ireland,' he writes. If O'Neill's figures are even close to being accurate, then he is right to claim that the role of eviction in the creation of the catastrophe is central. Many in England, including Trevelyan, viewed the potato blight as providential (and this has been used to explain their inactivity), but the higher figure for evictions can only mean that the landlords, including some who were members of the administration, were far more active than many historians suggest.

The only response to O'Neill's paper has been a brief and approving reference in an essay by Cormac O'Gráda in his *Black '47 and Beyond*. Besides changing our view on the role of evictions, O'Neill's work helps to copperfasten the notion that there are wild divergences not only in views and analyses of the Famine, but in the presentation of the most basic matters. The idea that O'Neill is multiplying Daly's figures for 1846, 1847 and 1848 by a factor of four or five, and is close to doubling those of Vaughan and Foster, makes it clear that no one has yet developed a methodology on how to arrive at the most basic calculations using the source material.

'At best,' O'Neill writes, 'the numbers of Famine evictions will remain a matter of approximation rather than accurate recording.' Nevertheless, he also writes: 'It seems hardly credible that historians could have such widely diverging views on the numbers evicted from 1846 to 1854.' O'Neill's work is a useful beginning. It is unfortunate that the lecture was published so long after it was delivered and so long after the main body of work to mark the 150th anniversary of the Famine.

None the less, any future work on the Famine will have to take account of it. W.E. Vaughan has written that 'emotion may have caused the exaggeration that seemed to accompany estimates of the number of evictions'. O'Neill, on the other hand, writes: 'Evictions were associated with the Great Famine in folk memory and given the likely scale of those evictions, this is understandable.'

Eamon de Valera, who came to power in the Irish Free State in 1932, was deeply concerned that because of emigration and social change a whole sense of the past was being lost in Ireland, that customs and stories were dying out, and the memory of events like the Famine was fading. In 1935 he set up the Irish Folklore Commission, which organised the work of both professional and voluntary folklore collectors. (In the early 1940s, in the absence of any British interest, de Valera organised employees of the Folklore Commission to go to the Isle of Man and record the last Manx speakers; the Commission also employed Calum MacLean, brother of the poet Sorley MacLean, to collect folklore in the Scottish Highlands.)

The folklore collection which resulted is now housed at University College Dublin. It comprises 3,500 bound volumes and more than 1,000 boxes of unbound material, plus a collection of sound recordings and

40,000 photographs. The collectors were encouraged to keep diaries of their time in the field and these are also housed in the archive.

Memories of the Famine come to us in three ways in the collection. First, through the ordinary work of the collectors, more valuable the closer it dates to 1935. Second, through a questionnaire sent to individuals throughout the country (including the North) in 1945. These individuals then collected information in their locality. Third, through material collected by school-children, aged between eleven and fourteen, in a special one-off folklore project in the Free State in 1937 and 1938, which included material on the memory of the Famine. This material consists of 1,100 volumes with 400 pages per volume. In his essay 'Famine Memory' in Black '47 and Beyond Cormac O'Gráda writes:

At its best [the material resulting from the 1945 questionnaire] is very rich, and the sheer bulk of the Folklore Commission's contribution is remarkable. Its 1945 questionnaire alone yielded over thirty-five hundred pages of material, mostly handwritten, from over five hundred informants. The average age of the informants was seventy-three to seventy-four years. Only one or two were old enough to remember the famine, but most had known close relatives or neighbours who had lived through it.

In the history of the Famine commissioned by de Valera, the final essay by Roger McHugh makes use of this material. It is significant that McHugh was a literary critic and not an historian. The truth of his chapter, he writes, is 'the truth, heard from afar, of the men and women who were caught up, uncomprehending and frantic, in that disaster'. Almost all Irish historians of the Famine have been uneasy about this 'truth, heard from afar'. One of the reasons for this, Cormac O'Gráda points out, is the plethora of documentary source material on the Famine. The case for using folk material is therefore 'less pressing'. But there are, he allows, other reasons, and these centre on the idea that myth and fact are arch-enemies; what the Folklore Commission collected was myth and what the historians sought to find was fact.

In his essay 'Irish History and Irish Mythology', published in 1977, T. W. Moody wrote:

But if 'history' is used in its proper sense of a continuing, probing, critical search for truth about the past, my argument would be that it is not Irish history but Irish mythology that has been ruinous to us and may prove even more lethal. History is a matter of facing the facts of the Irish past, however painful some of them may be; mythology is a way of refusing to face the historical facts.

Seamus Deane quotes the above passage in *Strange Country* and then writes: 'The discourse of the historian is taken to be a record of the world of objective facts; any elision or distortion of these produces "myth". Such a discourse, which claims for itself a fundamental realism through which things as they really are or were could be presented in a narrative, depends upon a narrator who is not implicated.' Most Irish historians from the 1970s onwards were liberals who wanted a non-sectarian, post-nationalist, pro-European Ireland; most of them grew to believe, innocently, that this was not a political position but a matter of common sense; they genuinely believed – and some still do – that this enabled them to write history impartially. They were, in any case, united in their common sense against material collected in 1945 about events a hundred years earlier being taken as seriously as institutional records.

The folklore material presents us with a problem, no matter what our views on nationalism, Europe or sectarianism. Cormac O'Gráda writes:

Though memories recounted much later may fail to reveal the true feelings of those at risk, they may capture them better than the standard documentary sources. Moreover, folklore is also about normative beliefs and semi-public attitudes, as exchanged between people – an important topic for famine historiographers. At its best the record [in the archive of the Folklore Commission] is vivid, eloquent and compelling.

He adds: 'Yet, ironically, Irish historians remain unconvinced of the value of this source.' O'Gráda offers a good reason for this in showing that the folklore is 'often – consciously or subconsciously – selective, evasive and apologetic'. It is of no use, he points out, for statistics or even basic facts and figures.

When you see the words vivid, eloquent and compelling and the words selective, evasive and apologetic all used to describe the same thing, you can feel the ghost of Maria Edgeworth's Thady of *Castle Rackrent* hovering over you in the company of all the other unreliable narrators in literary history and you realise that you are in very slippery territory indeed. The greatest champion of these Irish narrators whose voices were collected by the Folklore Commission has been the broadcaster Cathal Póirtéir, who has produced the only book on the subject, *Famine Echoes*, based on a series of radio programmes. 'Even where these traditions [as outlined in the folklore collection] seem to depart from historical facts, they may maintain a functional value as examples to reinforce the cultural norms or ideals of the community, of how it was felt that, for example, kindness would be rewarded and lack of kindness punished. Many of these formalised narratives predated the Great Famine of the 1840s; some of them can be identified in international oral tradition, while others have only a localised currency,' Póirtéir writes in his introduction.

Póirtéir is referring here to the large number of stories about people who behaved well in the Famine and were themselves miraculously rewarded. 'To a large extent the legends give us a picture of how people would have liked the world to be, express moral and religious values, and are a mechanism which helped communities deal with the horrors that surrounded them.'

The problem is that beside these legends in the folklore collection are accounts of the Famine which read as though they are true, and the narrator believed them and expected the collector to believe them. Question 2 in the 1945 questionnaire was: 'Please write down any stories or traditions you can find locally about the following: Famine deaths, burials, graves, graveyards; the cholera in your district; local fever hospitals at the time.' Clearly, no one who answered the questionnaire had witnessed any of the burials, but it is equally clear that many who had witnessed the burials would talk about it – and the talk would be vivid, eloquent and compelling rather than selective, evasive and apologetic. This is not to say that things were not added, made up or left out. But if you were writing a chapter on burial in a history of the Famine, this material would probably be a most useful, if not the most useful, source.

If you flick at random through the answers to question 2, all in clear handwriting, a good deal in Irish, you realise that in the chaos and changing circumstances of those years, there was no system for burial. It varied from place to place and time to time. 'They were buried without coffins on the spot where they were found as the living were too weak to carry them to a churchyard.' Or: 'All day long carts rumbled along carrying corpses to the graveyard. These were uncoffined and stared out at the passers by in a most discomforting manner.' Or: 'There were so many deaths that they opened big trenches through the graveyards and when they were full of dead they filled them in.'

There are a good number – it is hard to say how many, a great deal of systematic work remains to be done on the folklore archive – of accounts of people being buried alive. 'Some man from Carry … was burying his wife that time and the man noticed some movement in the coffin, and took the lid off and his wife was there wondering who she was.' This may indicate embellished talk around the fire at night in the years after the Famine, rather than a matter of fact, although it may, on the other hand, be a matter of fact. (Cormac O'Gráda quotes one of these accounts and calls it 'plausible'; I found none of the ones I came across plausible, but all of them chilling and as 'convincing' as anything in Sheridan le Fanu or Bram Stoker.) In any case, it cannot be 'dismissed' as myth; perhaps, instead, we should use the term 'raised to the level' of myth (*pace* T. W. Moody) and raise it accordingly as part of the dark memories and stories passed to the next generation by those who had witnessed scenes which remain for us almost unimaginable. Of course, all these accounts may be totally true.

The folklore archive on the Famine can, then, be anything you want it to be: it can be studded with legends and tales; it can be full of information which should be treated as almost primary source; it is a history of memory in Ireland after 1935; it should be consulted by all historians who write about the Famine; it should be consulted by literary critics.

It remains, however, an invaluable treasure trove. It is also full of tricks, as in the following answer to question 2 about burial during the Famine by a resident of Boyle in County Roscommon in 1945: 'Some of them were wrapped in a sheet and buried. At times a large number of dead bodies were placed in a grave together. No one wished to go near the bodies lest they themselves should take the fever. In some of the districts which had escaped the ravages of the fever, coffins were seen floating through the air.'

For any Irish historian, young or old, however deeply or lightly 'implicated', to use Seamus Deane's word, the last sentence here poses a serious problem: How can the first three sentences be taken as evidence about burial rites during the Famine, since the last cannot? Does not the last sentence fatally undermine the credibility of the first three? Yet the last helps us to understand how, when people talked about the Famine, superstition and Gothic fantasy were always close to hand. And the first three fit into other accounts. But it is easy to imagine the historian reading these four sentences in the Department of Irish Folklore in University College Dublin, sighing in exasperation and perhaps relief, closing the book and gratefully and dutifully going back to the study of Poor Law records, private correspondence, Cabinet minutes and contemporary newspapers in order to understand what happened in Ireland during the Great Famine.

Who emigrated in these years? How many got away? 'Nothing,' the Earl of Clanricarde wrote to Russell in December 1846, 'can effectually and immediately save the country without an extensive emigration. And I have not met in Town, or in Country, a reflecting man who does not entertain more or less the same opinion.' W.S. Trench, Lord Lansdowne's agent, wrote: 'Nothing but the successive failures of the potato could have produced the emigration which will, I trust, give us room to become civilised.' In his essay on Irish emigration in the book commissioned by de Valera, Oliver MacDonagh states that two million people left Ireland permanently from 1845 to 1855. 'The cottier class had virtually disappeared. The number of holdings under one acre had dropped from 134,000 to 36,000 ... the number of persons per square mile ... had fallen from 355 to 231; and the average productivity had risen greatly. In short the modern revolution in Irish farming had begun.'

In those years, people who were utterly destitute left the country; so did larger farmers who sold up and took what capital they could with them. 'From the famine onwards,' David Fitzpatrick writes, 'male and female emigrants were quite evenly balanced. Boys and girls alike swarmed out of every parish, every social stratum, and almost every household, systematically thinning out the fabric of Irish society.'

About a million people left, according to Fitzpatrick, between 1846 and 1850. 'The scale of that flight,' he writes, 'was unprecedented in the history of international migration.' Of those who left, 40,000 received subsidies from the landlord or the state. Major Denis Mahon in Roscommon helped his 'surplus' tenants to emigrate, his agent having informed him that the 2,400 people occupying his 2,100 acres produced only one third of the food needed for their support. He spent £14,000 on the project, having worked out that the cost of sending them to America was lower than keeping them as paupers for one year. A quarter of his tenants died at sea; the medical officer at Grosse Ile outside Quebec said that the survivors were the most wretched and diseased he had ever seen. Within a few months, Denis Mahon was murdered as a reprisal for this.

Emigrants in the early years of the Famine sent money back so that others could follow them. In 1850 a million pounds in remittances flowed back into Ireland. 'Hard-headed English economists,' Fitzpatrick writes, 'were bewildered by the seemingly unforced generosity and good sense of a people whom they had so often chastised for their imprudence, indiscipline and irresponsibility.' Many emigrants walked to the nearest port and found the cheapest exit; often they had no provisions or spare cash. 'It was cheaper to travel to Canada,' Daly writes, 'than to the United States because Canadian vessels were subject to less regulation, so Canada became the most common destination. Once arrived, those who were in fit condition walked across the border into the United States.'

By 1851 there were nearly a million people of Irish birth living in the US. Others, however, went to Britain, either as a final destination or as a first stop. In Black '47: Britain and the Famine Irish Frank Neal states that during eleven months of 1847 almost 300,000 people arrived in Liverpool from Ireland. Of these, 116,000 were 'half-naked and starving'. Conditions on the journey were dreadful. Neal quotes a contemporary report: the deck passengers

were generally crowded around the funnel of the steamer or huddled together in a most disgraceful manner; and as they have not been used to sea voyages, they get sick, and perfectly helpless, and covered with the dirt and filth of each other. I have seen the sea washing over the deck of a steamer I came over in, completely drenching the unfortunate people.

The immigrants brought typhus fever with them. 'Overwhelming opinion among the English, lay, medical, local and national, was that fever was an Irish import,' Neal writes. 'Certainly, the evidence is that the majority of victims were Irish.' In February 1847 the Home Secretary was informed that 88 per cent of the patients in the Liverpool fever hospitals were Irish. Relations between the immigrants and their hosts were not helped by the Irish custom of waking the dead. William Duncan, Liverpool's Medical Officer of Health, wrote to the Health Committee, begging to direct their 'attention to the objectionable custom of retaining the bodies of the dead, especially those who have died of infectious fevers, in the sleeping rooms of the living'.

Duncan developed strong views on the Irish, who, he said, were just as 'contented amidst dirt and filth, and close confined air, as in clean and airy situations'. The Select Vestry in Liverpool was told in March 1847 that

amongst a certain number of individuals in a cellar in Bent Street, it was reported that four were lying down in one bed, with fever, that 24 grown-up young men and their sisters were sleeping in a filthy state in the room; and that 14 persons were sleeping in another filthy place. 36 persons were found huddled together in a room elsewhere and eight had died of fever in one house.

Herman Melville visited Liverpool at this time and has a description of the city in his novel *Redburn: His First Voyage*:

It seemed hard to believe that such an array of misery could be furnished by any town in the world. Old women, rather mummies, drying up with slow starving and age; young girls, incurably sick, who ought to have been in the hospital; sturdy men with the gallows in their eyes, and a whining lie in their mouths; young boys, hollow-eyed and decrepit; and puny mothers, holding up puny babes in the glare of the sun, formed the main features of the scene.

Nathaniel Hawthorne, who was also staying in Liverpool, had a rather different attitude to the Irish on the docksides: 'The people are as numerous as maggots in cheese; you behold them, disgusting, and all moving about, as when you raise a plank or log that has long lain in the ground, and find many vivacious bugs and insects beneath it.'

By 1847 the arrivals in Quebec were also the cause of considerable alarm. Between 15 May and 17 June more than 2,000 people died at the quarantine station at Grosse Ile. On 31 May, with no further facilities on the island, forty vessels were at anchor in the St Lawrence. 'Thousands had still to lie on damp and open spaces,' according to MacDonagh, 'dying "like fish out of water", among the stones and mud flats of the beaches.' Eventually, fever victims were sent upriver, spreading typhus 'from Quebec to Montreal and farther west ... When the Irish arrived, people fled from Toronto and Kingston into the countryside.' By the end of 1847, 20,000 immigrants to Canada had died, 30 per cent of the entire Irish immigration. Most of the able-bodied who survived went south and settled in the United States. Although 80 per cent of them were of rural origin, only 6 per cent settled in the countryside; the rest remained in the cities. As you can imagine, historians are hesitant about figures for deaths at sea during these years, but Fitzpatrick states that 'shipboard mortality seldom exceeded one in fifty'.

The Famine had run its course; and another million people would emigrate over the next two decades. 'The Famine's part in improving the lot of most people who survived is indisputable,' O'Gráda writes in Ireland: A New Economic History 1780–1939. 'The impressive rises in tobacco, tea and sugar consumption were largely due to higher incomes ... The trends in literacy and housing quality also imply betterment after the Famine ... Life expectancy, under forty years on the eve of the Famine, had reached fifty years by the early 1870s.' The Irish language, according to Roy Foster, 'was increasingly abandoned; a large proportion of emigrants came from Irish-speaking areas, and those left behind were not anxious to preserve it. Its eradication was the achievement of ambitious parents as much as of English-speaking schoolteachers.' It was in decline in any case before the Famine, but the Famine accelerated the process. Three million spoke Irish in 1845; two million in 1851.

It is difficult to imagine Ireland in detail before or during the Famine. Once Pugin's cathedral was finished in Enniscorthy, in 1847 or 1848, it was possible to see the town clearly: if I were to set a novel in the years after its building – the years after the Famine – I would not have to do much research. The cathedral is the beginning of real time: what happened before it is history.

The Famine only comes close when you bring it close: when you read about it, when you see a list of names, or when you start thinking about evictions or half-naked people on the decks of ships being soaked by the waves, or when you hear a song about it, or see a mass grave, or a road built during those years, or read some soundbite by an English administrator or politician. In *Heathcliff and the Great Hunger*, Terry Eagleton asks: 'Where is the Famine in the literature of the Revival? Where is it in Joyce?' He goes on: 'If the Famine stirred some to angry rhetoric, it would seem to have traumatised others into muteness. The event strains at the limit of the articulable, and is truly in this sense an Irish Auschwitz.'

After Adorno, no more Adornos. It is possible that Eagleton himself knows that his last statement is not true 'in this sense' or any other. No one was traumatised into muteness who did not witness the events. But he goes on to make what seems to me a crucial point: 'Part of the horror of the Famine is its atavistic nature – the mind-shaking fact that an event with all the premodern character of a medieval pestilence happened in Ireland with frightening recentness.' I think that this 'premodern' quality puts the Famine beyond the reach of writers who came after it; and the speed with which society transformed itself – and perhaps the arrival of the camera – made the history of 1846, 1847 and 1848 in Ireland a set of erasures rather than a set of reminders. I know that there is a small body of imaginative writing about the Famine: Liam O'Flaherty's novel *Famine* is one, and there are echoes in works by Carleton and Yeats, but the two most recent works which refer to it, Patrick Kavanagh's long poem 'The Great Hunger' (1942) and Tom Murphy's play *Famine* (1968), are much more concerned with the contemporary world, with the spiritual and emotional famine of their own times, as Fintan O'Toole has pointed out, even though Murphy's play is set in the Famine years. For Joyce and for many other writers, the Famine was too distant, and the world that grew out of it too interesting and close and dramatic. As Seamus Deane writes in *Strange Country: Modernity and Nationhood in Irish Writing since 1790*, the literature and the politics of the Irish Revival achieved 'the remarkable feat of ignoring the Famine and rerouting the claim for cultural exceptionalism through legend rather than through history'. For Yeats, Lady Gregory and others, the invocation of an ancient, heroic Ireland was more powerful and less limiting than trying, as Seamus Deane puts it, 'to maintain the position that a traditional culture had been destroyed while making the integrity of that culture a claim for political independence'.

The book which made all the difference came out in 1962. It was Cecil

Woodham-Smith's *The Great Hunger: Ireland 1845–49*. It was a bestseller in Ireland at the time of publication and still sells well. In the United States it topped *Time* magazine's bestseller list for several weeks. This was the book that de Valera was waiting for. When Woodham-Smith came to Dublin to lecture, de Valera, by this time President of Ireland, attended. Later, after she was awarded an honorary degree by the National University of Ireland, de Valera gave a dinner in her honour and invited his old-time comrades from the struggle for independence and the Civil War. 'Though not an academic historian, Woodham-Smith was a formidable researcher,' O'Gráda writes. 'Much of her work is based on previously unused archival material.' In general, however, historians have a low opinion of her book. It is 'a highly dramatic and emotive picture of the famine', according to Daly. F.S.L. Lyons detected 'an attitude of mind which is not, in the deepest sense, historical'. Foster called her 'a zealous convert'.

Her crisp style belongs to another age. It is full of certainties and judgements about matters which have since been surrounded with qualifications and altered by shifting perspectives. She presents pen portraits of her protagonists – 'Trevelyan's qualities of rectitude, industry and complacency were not calculated to win popularity' – of a kind that is now frowned on. Her work is readable – something which later historians of the Famine have tried hard not to be. Beady-eyed, she tells it like a story. She ends chapters with cliff hangers. (Chapter 1 ends: 'Meanwhile, in 1844, a report was received that in North America a disease, hitherto unknown, had attacked the potato crop.') Her tone is English to the core, a cross between Margaret Thatcher and A.S. Byatt: she knows the difference between right and wrong (a matter which is still hotly debated in Ireland), and she knows a bad man when she sees one. Russell and Trevelyan are villains. If she relies too much on the study of personalities, her command of detail, her insistence on the cruelty of those in charge and the misery of those who suffered, and her ability to structure the narrative, account for the book's extraordinary impact.

Nobody will be able to write like that again. Reading *The Great Hunger* is like reading Georgian poetry while knowing that a new, fractured, 'modern' poetics is on the way. And in 1983 the historians' equivalent of *The Waste Land* appeared. It, too, was written by a foreigner. His name was Joel Mokyr. He was an American economic historian with no apparent Irish connections, and his book was called *Why Ireland Starved*. As Joseph Lee has written in his essay 'The Famine as History', Mokyr was not concerned, as Irish historians were, to provide 'ammunition for IRA interpretations of Irish history': 'He came to the topic mainly as an inviting case-study in economic underdevelopment, and in the relationship between population and development ... [His] reputation did not depend on the approval of peer groups in the history departments of either Irish or British universities ... He followed the figures where they took him.' They took him to the conclusion that more than a million people died in the Famine, twice the number proposed by Irish historians at the time. Mokyr also put forward the idea that there were 400,000 'averted births' because of the Famine. No Irish historian took up this matter: in 1983 an emotional debate was raging over 'the right to life of the unborn', and we heard enough about the unborn to do us all for a lifetime – only an outsider could have wanted us to contemplate the unborn of the Famine. Contemplating those who lived was proving hard enough.

As the 150th anniversary of the Famine approached, a quantity of books on the subject began to appear, some of which are listed here. A number were written in the shadow of Irish nationalism which, as we all know, had a fresh outing in Ireland after the IRA embarked on its campaign in the North in the early 1970s. Irish history, the old story of Ireland, was once more being used as a weapon to stir political emotions. The fastidiousness of Daly's approach should probably be seen in this context, while the approach of others – notably Christine Kinealy in *This Great Calamity* – is an effort to set the record straight and unrevise the revisionists.

Nothing is settled in Ireland. The years of Famine commemoration made this clear. For some, the silence surrounding the Famine and the attempt of Irish historians to remain cool about it are examples of denial, and only serve to show the importance of the Famine in the Irish psyche. Primary among these is the *Irish Times* columnist John Waters, who wrote in 1994:

Like so many other matters of vital importance to our condition, [the Famine] has been divided into a set of false opposites, on the one hand those who say that it was never as bad as we had been led to believe, and on the other, those who see the issue as a handy stick to beat the tribal drum. In between these polarised positions is the truth of our situation, a consciousness filled with grief and pain which has no way of expressing itself except through anger and escapism.

During her presidency, Mary Robinson spoke regularly about the Famine and the need to come to terms with it. In 1991, she became patron of the Famine Museum in Strokestown, County Roscommon, the home of Denis Mahon, who had paid for his surplus tenants to emigrate. In 1994 she visited Grosse Ile, where so many died in quarantine. She regarded the legacy of the Famine as central to the Irish experience, and because she carried no nationalist baggage (she had resigned from the Irish Labour Party over the Anglo-Irish Agreement in 1985) her tone was new. She managed to present the communal forgetting of the Famine victims as part of the general marginalisation of the weak in Ireland and suggested it was something we should think about in the 1990s.

In the early part of the decade, the Irish government set up a Famine Commemoration Committee with a budget of £750,000. Some of this money was used for the renovation of Famine graveyards, which dot the countryside; more than £100,000 was assigned to projects in the Third World. A hundred thousand pounds was given to historians to fund further research. History, you could be forgiven for thinking, was repeating itself, but this interpretation is too simple. In 1996, the four historians who oversaw the project – David Dickson, Fitzpatrick, Daly and O'Gráda – had distinguished track records in the study of famine and emigration, unlike the supervisors of the earlier project. They planned for three research assistants to carry out a study of eight Poor Law Unions; and five years on, a good deal of new, detailed information is available. This is not local history, which was already abundant, but a systematic attempt to explore all the available archives, noting variations and identifying patterns. But how should this be written up or placed in a narrative? Who will do it? What tone will they take? It is unlikely that the fruits of this work will be a masterpiece of historical writing.

Of all the recent publications on the Famine, two books are, however, masterpieces. Both offer microscopic examinations of tiny, almost fragmented areas rather than sweeping narratives of the Famine years. Both, interestingly, attempt what has not been much attempted before in Ireland: to write history from the perspective of those who were not administrators or politicians or landlords. One is David Fitzpatrick's *Oceans Of Consolation: Personal Accounts of Irish Migration to Australia* and the other is Robert James Scally's *The End of Hidden Ireland: Rebellion, Famine and Emigration.*

Fitzpatrick's book is

based on 111 letters, of which 55 were sent to Australia and 56 to Ireland. The letters range in length from a single line to 12 pages, the mean length being about eight hundred words (enough to fill four sides of a folded sheet). The sequences vary from two to 15 letters, only occasionally including correspondence in both directions. They were sent between 1843 and 1906, with a heavy concentration on the 1850s and 1860s.

The letters are not cut or edited. Each set of correspondence is introduced with as much detail as is available, both in Ireland and Australia, about the people who wrote them, the places they came from and where they went, their families, their associates. *Oceans Of Consolation* is a book of studied tracings, with enough material to give us a picture not only of the context but of the character of the people who wrote the letters. Fitzpatrick compares himself to a sub-postmistress, 'conversant with background and career, alert to gossip, but often shaky on detail', opening these letters.

The focus of his book, he writes, 'is upon the vernacular of the steerage class'. A good deal of the writing has that strange immediacy and clarity and sense of a living, speaking voice which you can get from letters that are not self-consciously literary. But there is always a literary element: you realise that much is being artfully withheld, that a long paragraph of news or opinions about Australia is there to disguise something else, deep feelings about home, or regrets, or other longings and attachments. When you come across a sentence like 'I hope I never shall dye until I see yea' or 'Dont ye be frightened about us', written from Australia in 1856 in an otherwise cheerful passage all about friends and neighbours, you realise that these must have been hard letters to write and hard to read when they arrived.

Robert Scally's *The End of Hidden Ireland* also involves an ingenious trawling through the archives to attempt a portrait of the people for whom men like Engels and Carlyle had such contempt. It is about Ballykilcline, County Roscommon, where the land on which a small community of around 500 men and women lived suddenly came into the possession of the Crown, in 1836, and for more than a decade the tenants paid no rent. The nearest landlord was Denis Mahon. On both counts, a good deal of attention was focused on these tenants, who were eventually evicted and offered assistance to emigrate. Scally slowly evaluates the wealth of archive material about the community, while supplying a great deal of background about land-holding and emigration.

The book is at times frustrating: it is like watching television with the sound down. Ballykilcline was clearly a community with its own dynamics; most people spoke Irish; some were bilingual, but they left nothing in writing except petitions. Their voices are missing, and after 1847 they disappear into America, some dying or vanishing on the way, and the place they came from as good as disappears from the map. At Westminster, Lord Monteagle described them as 'a mass of destitute paupers'. Scally's narrative, despite its problems, has brought us close enough to them, and to the intricate hierarchies and semi-clandestine affinities within their community, to feel almost offended at Monteagle's words. His book is an account of a small, interesting rebellion in the Irish backlands, the tenants wily and sharp enough to get away with not paying rent, as the forces of the state and the potato blight move slowly and inexorably towards them. Just as Euclides Da Cunha's *Rebellion in the Backlands* became Mario Vargas Llosa's novel *The War of the End of the World*, so *The End of Hidden Ireland* awaits its novelist. Fitzpatrick's *Oceans Of Consolation*, on the other hand, has the depth and narrative range of a novel.

It is easy for Scally to re-create the lives and adventures of the middlemen who operated on behalf of the state and the landlord. These were the Catholics who thrived while the land was cleared. The letters and reports that survive demonstrate once more the self-interest which characterised the ruling class in Ireland in these years. Scally writes: 'Both lord lieutenants of the time, Clarendon and Bessborough, held lands in Ireland and were highly alert to the potential for violence in the situation ... The dramatic rise in the number and severity of criminal sentences while the famine lasted gives a harrowing testimony to their intentions in policing Ireland in the midst of famine.'

On 31 May 1997, the new British Prime Minister, Tony Blair, apologised for the Famine. 'I am glad,' he said, 'to have this opportunity to join with you in commemorating all those who suffered and died during the Great Irish Famine.' He spoke of 'deep scars' and the failure of a government which 'stood by while a crop failure turned into a massive human tragedy'. The brief speech ended with a call to 'celebrate the resilience and courage of those Irish men and women who were able to forge another life outside Ireland, and the rich culture and vitality they brought with them. Britain, the US and many Commonwealth countries are richer for their presence.'

This was originally written to be read by Tony Blair on a video-link at a commemoration of the Great Famine, funded in part by the Irish Government, which was held in Cork on the June Bank Holiday weekend of 1997, but the plan was abandoned and the apology was read out by the actor Gabriel Byrne. It struck the right note for the commemoration, which was known as the Great Irish Famine Event – it was, in fact, a rock concert – and billed 'as a celebration of triumph over disaster'. (Bob Dylan was to be there, but had a heart attack just beforehand.)

This was the main public commemoration of the Famine in Ireland. The country grew economically in the second half of the nineteenth century on the strength of the land clearances, and had not bothered much about the Famine legacy for reasons which I have explained. In the second half of the 1990s it was experiencing a sustained boom. Clearly, we wanted to celebrate our 'skills and talents', our 'rich culture and vitality', as Blair would have it. On the other hand, the event was so crass that one wondered if it had not been entirely imagined by Jonathan Swift or Paul Durcan, whose poem 'What Shall I Wear, Darling, to the Great Hunger?' is included in Tom Hayden's book *Irish Hunger*.

During the week before the Bank Holiday concert, John Waters wrote:

This weekend, courtesy of the Minister [Avril Doyle, junior minister at the Department of the Taoiseach] and her Government of amnesia, the Irish public will be invited, as paying spectators, to commodify the destruction of our ancestors and offer it up at the altar of tourism in 'one great big party'. In this she has created the perfect metaphor for the Ireland of the Celtic Tiger, a travesty of nature built upon the graves of its dead.

'If it is to happen at all,' Waters said, the occasion 'should indeed be solemn and terrible'. (No wonder Bob Dylan had a heart attack.)

In the US, on the 150th anniversary, the Governor of New York, George Pataki, signed a Bill which would legally require high school students to study the Great Famine. 'History teaches us,' he said, 'that the Great Hunger was not the result of a massive Irish crop failure, but rather a deliberate campaign by the British to deny the Irish people the food they needed to survive.' In an article in the *Washington Post* on 17 September 1997 Timothy Guinnane, associate professor of economics at Yale, wrote:

Several states have mandated that the Great Irish Famine of 1845–1850 be taught in their high schools as an example of genocide, sometimes in courses originally intended for the study of the Holocaust. More states are considering enacting similar measures. These mandates reflect the efforts of a small number of Irish American leaders who have pushed this line for ideological reasons.

The Irish Famine Curriculum Committee had already submitted a document to the New Jersey Commission on Holocaust Education in 1996. It was intended for inclusion in the Holocaust and Genocide Curriculum at secondary level. The text is full of emotional language, selective quotation and a vicious anti-English rhetoric. It asserts, despite all the evidence to the contrary, that Ireland remained a net exporter of food during the Famine. It is as shocking in its carelessness and its racism as the London *Times* editorials were about Ireland during and after the Famine. It is clear that the authors of the document want us all to be victims together. When they set foot in the Ireland of the Celtic Tiger, they will be in for a shock. Cecil Woodham-Smith, according to the Curriculum Committee, was 'considered the pre-eminent authority on the Irish Famine'. Luckily for us all, this is no longer the case. Some scholars, however, have taken a more sober approach to the task of inventing a curriculum for American schools. Professor Maureen Murphy of Hofstra University, the editor of Asenath Nicholson's *Annals of the Famine in Ireland* and one of the most thoughtful and serious writers on nineteenth-century Ireland, was awarded a grant by the New York State Education Department to develop a curriculum. Her team's lesson plans include the most fundamental questions about the Famine as well as a much broader context, such as comparisons with Indian famines and examination of the role of the Quakers in famine relief.

Slowly, then, a deeper understanding of the forces which caused the catastrophe in Ireland may begin to pervade the United States.

Fifty years after the Famine, in February 1895, Lady Gregory wrote to a friend:

The garden is like Italy, warm sunshine and many flowers out, wallflowers, grape hyacinths, violets and in the woods, primroses. I did a little ornamental planting yesterday, putting out copper beeches and laburnums raised from seed in my own nursery. I hope, if there are ever grandchildren, they will be grateful some day. Our people are paying rents and paying very well, and a policeman who came from Gort in the holidays to cut the boys' hair said that he was glad of the distraction, as they have absolutely nothing to do here now.

The scene is straight out of Chekhov in its innocence and melancholy and self-absorption, but there is no Lenin lurking in the undergrowth: the changes in Ireland came subtly and slowly. In a series of Land Acts, the old estates, which had been cleared of cottier tenants, were divided up, and the deeply conservative Catholic farmer class came into being. Lady Gregory's nephew John Shaw-Taylor was one of the architects of this legislation. By 1923 two million acres had been redistributed.

Around the mid-1890s, according to her diaries, Lady Gregory realised that 'the breaking of Parnell's power and his death' in 1891 had 'pushed politics into the background, and ... there came a birth of new hope and interests, as it were, a setting free of the imagination'. Ireland, then, could concentrate on myth and folklife and cultural de-Anglicisation rather than partisan politics, bitterness and economic argument. Poets, dramatists and dreamers could set the tone of the debate. And in the prosperous demesnes of the west, where a new, dreamy nationalism began to thrive, the events of the Famine had no place.

'THE CAPRICIOUS GROWTH OF A SINGLE ROOT'

Irish Famine Documents

When state relief failed, people were dependent on private philanthropy. Here the daughter of Captain Kennedy, the Poor Law inspector of the Kilrush Union, distributes clothing to the evicted, November 1849.

Foreword

One of the essential habits of English Victorian poetry is to move between a highly wrought, ornate diction and plain statement. In the poetry of Tennyson or Emily Brontë, Matthew Arnold or Gerard Manley Hopkins, the use of a flat, stark sentence or statement has an enormous power, can run through the poem like an electric shock, as all around it appear sweet cadence, poetic inversion or language which is artful and on display.

In *In Memoriam*, Tennyson writes:

> He is not here; but far away
> The noise of life begins again,
> And ghastly through the drizzling rain
> On the bald street breaks the blank day.

Or in *Felix Randal*, Hopkins begins the second stanza with a simple sentence: 'Sickness broke him.'

Or, perhaps most powerfully, Matthew Arnold begins *Dover Beach* with: 'The sea is calm tonight.' The sentence, itself, like the others quoted, is, of course, calm, but it also establishes itself as a special kind of truth, one with no embellishment, that can be trusted. With all of these poets, such clear diction often feels as though it has broken through, as though the voice suddenly tired of making the noise of art and was forced by the weight of what it wanted to say to make, in Tennyson's phrase, 'the noise of life'.

Any reading of contemporary documents relating to the catastrophe in Ireland in the late 1840s finds that this tension between language as a way of surrounding reality with artifice and the sudden breaking-through of pure bald statement is central. The Victorian politician, like the Victorian poet, finds for one moment the need to state something clearly. On 17 October 1845, for example, Lord Heytesbury, the Lord Lieutenant, wrote to Sir Robert Peel: 'These reports continue to be of a very alarming nature, and leave no doubt upon the mind but that the potato crop has failed almost everywhere.' Look at the rhythm of those last eight words: *that the potato crop has failed almost everywhere*. In neither its tempo, its meaning nor its tone does the phrasing allow prevarication. In its baldness and its artlessness it conceals nothing. And yet, like the lines from the poets, its very clarity and artlessness shock us.

Two years later Lord John Russell wrote to Lord Clarendon: 'It is quite true that landlords in England would not bear to be shot like hares or partridges by miscreants banded for murderous purposes.' Russell must have enjoyed writing that last sentence, relished its tone and structure. But then he had something urgent he wanted to say and he forgot his own talents as a sentence-shaper: 'But neither does any landlord in England turn out fifty persons at once, and burn their homes over their heads, giving them no provision for the future.' Suddenly, you can hear a voice clearly.

You read the official reports, then, for signs that there will be a tear in the cloak of official language. But those who witnessed what happened and were literate take a different tone. It is one you find in Thomas Hardy especially, but in Tennyson too: a tone of pure, flat statement which is lifted, surrounded with a short of awed, hidden, raw cadence so that you're never quite sure where the emotion is coming from.

Both Tennyson and Hardy are skilled at presenting the world in its exact detail, down to the tiniest thing. This mixture of flat description and someone desperately trying to describe the indescribable comes up again and again in first-hand accounts of the dead and the dying in Ireland in 1846 and 1847:

By the side of the western wall is a long, newly-made grave; by either gable are two of shorter dimensions, which had recently been tenanted; and near the hole that serves as a doorway is the last resting place of two or three children; in fact, this hut is surrounded by a rampart of human bones, which have accumulated to such a height in the threshold, which was originally on a level with the ground, is now two feet beneath it. In this horrible den, in the midst of a mass of human putrefaction, six individuals, males and females, labouring under most malignant fever, were huddled together, as closely as were the dead in the graves around.

Sometimes in these documents you turn a page and find another description of famine and pestilence, then you read on as though you know this story until you come to a phrase which startles you in a way that nothing in literature or poetry could. In March 1847 the *Mayo Constitution* published an account of the condition of Ballinrobe workhouse which was 'in the most awfully deplorable state, pestilence having attacked paupers, officers and all'.

In fact, this building is one horrible charnel house, the unfortunate paupers being nearly all the victims of a fearful fever, the dying and the dead, we might say, huddled together. The master has become the victim of this dread disease; the clerk, a young man whose energies were devoted to the well-being of the union, has been added to the victims; the matron, too, is dead; and the respected, and esteemed physician has fallen before the ravages of pestilence, in his constant attendance on the diseased inmates.

In all Victorian writing, it would be hard to find a phrase as effective, as astonishing in its stark truth as 'the matron, too, is dead'.

These documents that follow have not been chosen at random. They attempt to illustrate competing and complementary versions of the forces at work in Ireland in the 1840s. Part of the strangeness of Irish history is the way in which events remain wide open to interpretation. In 1898, for example, nationalist Ireland needed 1798 as a Catholic nationalist rebellion against the English, led by priests. In 1998, Europhile and semi-pluralist Ireland needed 1798 as a peasant rebellion led by Protestant intellectuals which had its roots in European rationalism. Each time the rebellion of 1798 lay down and let the waters of current politics wash over it. The Famine, too, remains open to interpretation. A selection of documents is capable of showing this, insisting on the impossibility of closure, now that a definitive narrative seems almost out of the question.

It is possible, on studying these documents, to agree with John Mitchel that 'the almighty indeed sent the potato blight, but the English created the Famine'. The writings of Trevelyan about famine and Ireland remain chilling and disturbing, as do newspaper reports and internal government documents. It is possible, also, to read the documents about savings and food prices and conclude that the Irish merchant classes and middlemen made a fortune out of the Famine, and that a whole new stable Ireland came into being on the ruins of the smallholding class. It is possible also to read these documents and scratch your head in wonder, indeed puzzlement, at some facts and figures, especially those relating to evictions, export of cattle and Poor Law rates collected. It is hard, on reading these documents, not to feel contempt for the landlord class, and even harder to understand that landlords everywhere have wanted the rent paid on time.

These documents, then, do nothing to settle the argument; instead, they establish its terms and its complexity. They offer a set of essential primary sources, selected for their variety and for the light they throw on contemporary events and attitudes, reactions and competing styles of discourse. They include facts and figures. Our own prejudices, mine and Diarmaid Ferriter's, should be very clear: we both recognise that no narrative now seems capable of combining the sheer scale of the tragedy in all its emotion and catastrophe, the complex society which surrounded it and the high politics which governed it. Any story of the Famine includes a clashing set of stories, few complete, most fragmented. This book allows the reader to understand the complex way in which the fragmentary past is both available to us through documents and distant from us because of our abiding interest in making sense of it.

C. T.

IRISH FAMINE DOCUMENTS

Selected and introduced by Diarmaid Ferriter

Note on the Text

Abbreviations

BBP: British Parliamentary Papers, Famine Series, Irish University Press
DP: Distress papers, Famine, National Archives of Ireland
NAI: National Archives of Ireland
NLI: National Library of Ireland
IFC: Irish Folklore Commission
RLFC: Relief Commission Papers, National Archives of Ireland
SFFP: Society of Friends [Quakers] Famine Papers, National Archives of
Ireland

Shortly after the appearance of the potato blight in 1845 the government directed the Irish Constabulary to ascertain the extent of the disease and report weekly on its progress. The following is a digest of their reports for the month of October.

1 October 1845

Clare: There will be no loss either from failure or disease in the early crop to reduce it below average. From all appearances the late crop will be unusually abundant; much more land under potatoes this year than formerly, chiefly from tracts hitherto uncultivated having been reclaimed.

Cork, East Riding: On the whole the crop appears above average. The failures are of a very limited extent.

Cork, West Riding: Most cheering upon the whole, notwithstanding very partial failures.

Donegal: No scarcity to be apprehended, although a partial failure in the subdistrict of Carrowkeel: Crop apparently healthy and fruitful; possibly some to spare.

Fermanagh: A probable deficiency of about one tenth of the whole.

Galway, West Riding: An abundant crop is expected: more so in some districts than the oldest inhabitants can remember.

Kerry: An average crop, although in some localities, particularly along the coast, there is a rot.

King's County: Crop partially injured by the frost (the only source of danger) but no serious apprehension throughout the country generally (all other crops fully average).

Wexford: A partial failure from rot (but it will be more than balanced by the very abundant oat crop).

17 October 1845

Armagh: The disease has increased to an alarming extent; of 112 lbs of 'Cork Reds' and 'sons of cups' dug out of some rich heavy land, 65lbs were bad and 47lbs unusuable. The failure has been less general in light soils and pieces of grain and meal have risen.

Cork: Fermoy: A meeting of the Poor Law Guardians held this day – present Lord Mountcashell and 26 other guardians – to consider the subject. The general opinion was that at least one third of the potatoes are unfit for food, but that the extent of the disease cannot be fully ascertained until all have been dug out and for some time pitted. An address agreed to be forwarded to the Lord Lieutenant praying that exportation may be prevented.

Down: Ballinahinch: About one fourth supposed to be destroyed. For upwards of a week however the disease has made no progress. Downpatrick much more alarming since the 7th instant, the 'cups' having in many instances become diseased. One third of the crop through the district believed to be destroyed. A quantity of 'black seedlings' was pitted ten days ago in apparently good condition and one third are this week found to be decayed.

King's County: Ferbane: The distemper has lately appeared in some parts of the district. Some parts are free from it.

Meath: Trim: Failure very general. In one field the labourers were obliged to give up digging from the disagreeable smell.

Wicklow: Rathdrum; Farmers are discovering that the disease is more serious, especially in the low ground, and about the sea, than was at first supposed.

Westmeath: Castletown: Scarcely a potato untouched by the disease.

Kilkenny: Johnstown: Crop more or less diseased throughout the district: on some farms nearly half quite rotten.

21 October 1845

Galway East: Ballygan: The Sub-Inspectors saw two fields of 16 and 13 acres in another part of the district and one of 10 acres near Ballygan. So bad that the poor people who rented the fields said they were not worth digging.

Navan: During the last week or ten days complaints of general failure are numerous. In many instances more than one third destroyed. Very few fields free from disease. Only two or three farmers have commenced to dig out their crop, most persons being of opinion that the longer they remain in the ground the less they are damaged.

Wexford County: The disease is daily becoming more alarming. In some places, the root has altogether disappeared, having melted into the earth, leaving the withered stalk behind. Everyone is selling off as fast as possible at low rates.

(NAI, RLFC. Z Series 213210-214130)

The responses to the initial appearance of the blight ranged from measured caution to outright alarm. Many local Guardians convened special meetings to discuss the impending crisis. The following was the response of the Lord Mayor of Cork on 10 October 1845.

May it please your excellency: the very great and it is to be feared well-founded alarm which the decay in the potatoe crop has produced among the people induces me to add to the number of communications which must have been made to your excellency, praying your excellency's attention to the state of agricultural produce along with other places in this part of the Kingdom. I do not my lord for a moment suppose that your excellency has omitted to procure prompt and early information on this all important subject, but I request that enquiries may avowedly and publicly [be] made by the government as to the present state and probable prospects of the great staple of Irish existence, so that seeing themselves cared for by those who are in authority they may be patient if they have to endure the severe visitation of scarcity of their only food. As to measures of remedy or precaution, it is not my province to suggest them. I am sure the government has already been prompt and ready to consider well a subject in which the health and peace of the nation is necessary involved.

I am your Lord, Your Excellency's humble servant,

Richard Dowden
Mayor of Cork

(NAI, RLFC, Z Series 2/13644)

By the middle of November 1845 the full extent of the crop failure was becoming apparent. The following was a resolution addressed to the Lord Lieutenant, Lord Heytesbury, by the Mansion House Committee, whose membership was composed of many notables from the Dublin Corporation and chaired by the Duke of Leinster and Lord Cloncurry.

... That we have ascertained beyond the shadow of doubt, that considerably more than one-third of the entire of the potato crop in Ireland has been already destroyed by the potato disease; and that such disease has not, by any means ceased its ravages, but, on the contrary, it is daily extending more and more; and that no reasonable conjecture can be formed with respect to the limits of its effects, short of the destruction of the entire remaining potato crop ... that our information upon the subject is positive and precise and is derived from persons living in all the counties of Ireland, from persons also of all political opinions and from clergymen of all religious persuasions. We are thus unfortunately able to proclaim to all the inhabitants of the British Empire, and in the presence of an all-seeing Providence, that in Ireland famine of a most hideous description must be immediate and pressing, and that pestilence of the most frightening kind is certain, and not remote, unless immediately prevented ... That we arraign in the strongest terms, consistent with personal respect to ourselves, the culpable conduct of the present administration, as well in refusing to take any efficacious measure for alleviating the present calamity with all its approaching hideous and necessary consequences; as also for the positive and unequivocal crime of keeping the ports closed against the importation of foreign provisions, thus either abdicating their duty to the people or their sovereign, whose servants they are, or involving themselves in the enormous guilt of aggravating starvation and famine, by unnaturally keeping up the price of provisions, and doing this for the benefit of a selfish class who derive at the present awful crisis pecuniary advantages to themselves by the maintenance of the oppressive Corn Laws ...That the people of Ireland, in their bitter hours of misfortune, have the strongest right to impeach the criminality of the ministers of the Crown, inasmuch as it has pleased a merciful Providence to favour Ireland in the present season with a most abundant crop of oats. Yet, whilst the Irish harbours are closed against the importation of foreign food, they are left open for the exportation of Irish grain, an exportation which has already amounted in the present season to a quantity nearly adequate to feed the entire people of Ireland, and to avert the now certain famine; thus inflicting upon the Irish people the abject misery of having their own provisions carried away to feed others, whilst they themselves are left contemptuously to starve ...

Signed John L. Arabin

Lord Mayor of Dublin

(Revd John O'Rourke, *The History of the Great Irish Famine* (Dublin, 1902) pp. 65–7)

Lord Heytesbury's reply to the deputation.

My Lord Mayor and gentlemen, – It can scarcely be necessary for me to assure you that the state of the potato crop has for some time occupied, and still occupies, the most anxious attention of the government. Scientific men have been sent over from England to co-operate with those of this country, in endeavouring to investigate the nature of the disease, and, if possible, to devise means to arrest its progress. They have not yet terminated their enquiries; but two reports have already been received from them, which have been communicated to the public. The government is also furnished with constant reports from the stipendiary magistrates and inspectors of constabulary, who are charged to watch the state of the potato disease, and the progress of the harvest. These vary from day to day, and are often contradictory. It will, therefore, be impossible to form an accurate opinion on the whole extent of the evil till the digging of the potatoes should be further advanced. To decide, under such circumstances, upon the most proper measures to be adopted, would be premature; particularly as there is reason to hope that, though the evil exists to a very great extent in some localities, in others it has but partially manifested itself.

There is no immediate pressure in the market. I will, however, lose no time in submitting your suggestions to the consideration of the Cabinet. The greater part of them can only be enforced by legislative enactment, and all require to be maturely weighed before they can be adopted. It must be clear to you, that in a case of such great national importance, no decision can be taken without a previous reference to the responsible advisers of the Crown ...

(O'Rourke, *History*, pp.56–7)

Many suggestions were made in the following months as to how best to cook potatoes, or methods of salvaging something edible from a virtually destroyed crop. The following suggestions were made to cottiers in County Tipperary.

Suggestions to Cottagers in Cooking their Potatoes

Commence with YOUR DISEASED POTATOES, by washing them well, then peel or scrape off the skins, carefully cutting out such parts as are discoloured; cut the large Potatoes to the size of the smaller ones, and steep them for a short time in salt and water.

Provide a few cabbage leaves (the white kind is the most suitable); steep them in cold water, then line the bottom and sides of a common metal or oven pot, with the wet leaves; pack it in, the peeled potatoes in layers, shaking salt and pepper over each layer until the vessel is nearly full; spread more wet cabbage leaves over them on a hot-hearth, or a moderate fire, as too hot a fire might be attended with risk.

The object of the above-mentioned method is, that the Potatoes should be cooked through the medium of their own moisture, instead of the usual mode of steaming or boiling them in water.

The following additions may be made by those who can afford to improve upon the above, by introducing sliced Onions, salt Herring, salt Butter, salt Pork, Lard or Bacon cut in slices, or small pieces, or Rice, previously boiled.

It would be found more economical, instead of peeling, to scrape off the skins of such Potatoes as are only slightly discoloured or altogether free from taint.

Those who have a Cow or Pigs to feed should collect the peelings and rejected portions of the Potatoes, steep them for some time in salt and water, then pack them in a metal pot, in layers, with cabbage leaves, sprinkling salt over each layer, and cook them as above directed; if found necessary, a little Bran or Oatmeal may be added.

Berryluskan, 1st December, 1845

(NAI, RLFC 3/1/676)

This letter, dated 23 October 1845, was written by Lennox Bigger from Dundalk, detailing his experiments to render diseased potatoes edible.

... Having, I confess, lost many sleepless hours respecting the *cause* and *effect* of the Rot in the Potato crop, it struck me to try if I could find out the first, and alleviate the latter, no person *now* can be called an *alarmist*, who says that a few fields in the kingdom have entirely escaped the contagion, and it is the Duty, as it should be the inclination of everyone to state what they feel would be a remedy for the evil. I gave up an entire day to trying experiments upon the *diseased Potatoes alone.* I got the full of a middle sized Pot of them peeled and boiled well, as soon as they came to a boil, I had the first water thrown off, cold water put on, and on the second water being put off (having previously boiled two salt herrings, the bones taken out), added them and had all *well pounded* together put in a small quantity of ground pepper and a little salt, I then sent for my Labourers twelve in number. I first, myself, tasted it, and made each of them do so, they all pronounced it '*very good*' and some eat heartily of it, all declaring they would pursue the plan and expressed themselves most thankful. I had a pot of Potatoes put down in the usual way with the skins on excepting the rotten part, and as before the first water being thrown off (which had such a bad smell, I would not allow it to be given to the pigs) and cold water added, *on the top* I put three salt herrings and boiled them on the Potatoes, and all being turned out in the usual way on the Riddle and the Herrings put on a plate in the middle, the family sat down to dinner, and I give their words 'only for the Herrings these Potatoes we could not eat'. I divided a barrel of Herrings among those Labouring Tenants according* to the number of their families from 90 to 120 each, and gave to each a paper of pepper, I gave Tin Graters to them for making starch, which I found the women *understood perfectly*, and I was happy to see some beginning to be used before I left them, I would be very glad to be able to state the result of these tryals, but am anxious to make those which I have made public, feeling that no time should be lost, not even a day, in giving these first results, and I say to all others, 'what you do do quickly.' Remember there are 9 months to come before a new crop can relieve, and all that can, should be done to make the present beneficial both for feeding and Seed.

Richmond, Dundalk, October 23rd, 1845

Lennox Bigger

*Note – I have ordered tryals to be made with mixing a Turnip or two to the champ and 2 or 3 onions in others. I intend also to try the starch which a gentleman stated would give 3lb of flour from the stone of Potatoes, 24lb from the Cwt. would be very valuable for rotted ones, would be 4s. per Cwt. at 2d. per lb.

The Barrel to get is what contains 9 Hundred, some (large) have only 6 cwt. The tin grater, a sheet tin cost 4d.

(NAI, RLFC 2/Z14658)

Composition of the Population of Ireland, 1841

Adult males	2,341,895
Adult females	2,529,660
Older children	977,020
Younger children	2,326,549
Total	8,175,124

(Census of Ireland for the Year 1841)

Number of Persons Holding Land, 1845

Acres	Number	Percentage
Less than 1	135,314	8.5
Less than 1 to 10	369,859	23.3
Less than 10 to 20	187,582	11.9
Less than 20 to 50	141,819	9.0
Above 50	70,441	4.4
Unclassified	30,433	1.9
Total landholders	935,448	59.0
Landless labourers	650,552	41.0
Total	1,586,000	100.0

Landless labourers and their dependents exceeded 2.25 million people. Cottiers and smallholders (under 10 acres) made up a further 1.75 million people.

Two-thirds of the workforce were dependent on agriculture in the 1840s while only one in seven of the population lived in towns and cities.

(Figures based on the Poor Law Returns for 1845, cited in Austin Bourke, 'The
Agricultural Statistics of the 1841 Census. A Critical Review', Economic History Review, 2nd
series, vol. XVIII (1965), pp. 377–81)

Potato Consumption per Day in Pre-Famine Ireland by Labourers, Cottiers and Smallholders' Families

Adult males	6.4 kg (14 lbs)
Adult females	5.1 kg (11.2 lbs)
Children 11–15 years	5.1 kg (11.2 lbs)
Children under 11 years	2.2 kg (4.9lbs)

(John Keating, *Irish Famine Facts* (Dublin, 1996), p. 9)

Average Potato Production in Ireland

Period	Potato Crop (thousands of tons)
Early 1840s	c.15,000
1847–56	4,423
1857–66	3,407
1867–76	3,361
1877–76	2,642
1887–96	2,740
1897–1906	2,647
1907–16	3,088
1917–26	2,976
1927–36	3,470
1937–46	4,116
1947–56	3,844

(Austin Bourke, 'The Visitation of God?' The Potato and the Great Irish Famine (Dublin, 1993), p. 55)

The response of the British government to the famine was particularly significant in the context of debates about the nature and future of Irish society and also the prevailing political and economic orthodoxies which underpinned British policy. A link between British radicals and the cause of Ireland was evident in the pre-famine decade in the writings of the radical journalist and editor of the Political Register William Cobbett, who visited Ireland in 1834 and ominously anticipated tragedy and conflict for the future of the island. But few, if any, could have anticipated the scale of the impending tragedy, despite previous Irish famines.

Ultimately, the famine was to highlight the link between relief policies and the land question in Ireland. The already well developed pre-famine debates over the duties and responsibilities of landed proprietors and the need for self-reliance on the part of tenants were further fuelled as were issues closely linked to contemporary debate such as free trade versus a protective economic regime. A new age of classical economists, like Nassau William Senior, were insistent that the cottier system needed to be swept aside in order to develop Irish agricultural resources. The anglicisation of Irish society through the introduction of large-scale capitalist farming was central to the vision of such economists, who maintained that the surplus population of Ireland was a problem which could only be rectified by consolidation of holdings and the conversion of the cottier class into wage labourers, though it was acknowledged by some that assistance would be needed in the short term.

The relief policies of the Tory Prime Minister at the onset of the Famine, Robert Peel, included a Relief Commission, established in November 1845 to organise food depots and reconstituted the following February. In November 1845 Peel and Goulburn, his Chancellor of the Exchequer, ordered that £100,000 be spent on buying Indian corn for secret shipment and storage in Ireland. It was sold cheaply when the price of food rose above a certain level, mainly to local relief committees, of which there were over 600 by the summer of 1846. In March 1846 a Public Works Act was passed to provide employment for those affected by the famine – the Office of Public Works (often referred to as the Board of Works) had been established in 1831 to co-ordinate relief work projects in Ireland and administer various public programmes.

Peel argued strongly for the repeal of the Corn Laws. He believed that precautionary and relief measures taken against the famine were inconsistent with agricultural protection, and that its removal was needed in order that food could be imported at the cheapest rate and England could be compensated for expenditure on Irish relief. The debate about ending agricultural protection also threw light on the need for social stability in the structure of rural Ireland, and although the Tory government initially resisted calls for increased coercive power, it was offered out of political expediency at a time when the repeal of the Corn Laws was threatened, amid staunch defence of the maintenance of the rights of property. Coercive measures were proposed by Peel in the context of acting as a deterrent and encouraging a self-regulating system of social relationships, the argument being that reform of the Irish land system was unattainable until agrarian crime was repressed. Peel's attempts to pass such legislation contributed to the downfall of his administration in June 1846.

Cobbett's warning to England after his visit to Ireland in 1834.

Gentlemen, it is impossible that Ireland can be suffered to remain in its present state! What! Vessels laden with provisions ready to sail for England, while those who have raised the provisions are starving on the spot where they raised them! What! Landlords living in England, having a 'RIGHT' to drive the King's subjects out of this island, on pain of starvation from hunger and from cold! What! Call upon England for meal and money to be sent in charity to save the people of Ireland from starving, and make the relieved persons *pay rent the same year!* What! Demand allegiance from a man whom you toss out upon the road, denying that he has any right to demand from any part of the community the means of sustaining life! ...What! Give to 349,000 of the English people as many representatives in Parliament as you give to the whole Irish nation, and bid the latter be content ...

(Denis Knight (ed.), *Cobbett in Ireland: A Warning to England* (London, 1984), pp. 210–11)

The assessment of economist Nassau Senior, before the famine.

Indolence – the last of the causes to which we have attributed the existing misery of Ireland – is not so much an independent source of evil, as the result of the combination of all the others ... The indolence of the agricultural labourer arises, perhaps, principally from his labour being almost always day-work, and in great measure a mere payment of a debt – a mere mode of working out his rent. That of the occupier may be attributed to a combination of causes. In the first place, a man must be master of himself to a degree not common even among the educated classes, before he can be trusted to be his own task-master ... The Irish occupier, working for a distant object, dependent in some measure on the seasons, and with no one to control, or even to advise him, puts off to-morrow what need not necessarily be done to-day – puts off to next year what need not be necessarily done this year, and ultimately leaves much totally undone ...

(Nassau Senior, 'Ireland', *Edinburgh Review* LXXIX (January, 1844), pp. 206–7)

Letter from Sir Robert Peel to Lord Heytesbury.

Drayton Manor, 15 October 1845

My Dear Lord Heytesbury,

The Accounts from Ireland of the potato crop, confirmed as thay are by your high authority, are very alarming ... [The] remedy is the removal of all impediments to the import of all kinds of human food – that is, the total and absolute repeal for ever of all duties on all articles of subsistence. I believe that, practically, there would be no alternative. To remit the duty on Indian corn expressly for the purpose of averting famine would make it very invidious to retain a duty on other species of corn more generally applicable to the food of man. You might remit nominally for one year; but who will re-establish the Corn Laws once abrogated, though from a casual and temporary pressure? I have good ground, therefore, for stating that the application of a temporary remedy to a temporary evil does in this particular instance involve considerations of the utmost and most lasting importance.

You must therefore send us from time to time the most authentic information you can. There is such a tendency in Ireland to disregard accuracy and to exaggerate, that one is unwilling to give hasty credence to Irish statements. There can, however, I fear, be no reason to doubt that the failure of the potato crop will be very general. Has the recent fine weather (which has, I presume, extended to Ireland) had a favourable effect? What is the price of potatoes in the different markets? Is that price rapidly increasing? I fear the lowness of price – even if it exist – might be no indication of abundance. There might be an undue quantity of inferior potatoes sent for sale, for fear of rapid decay if they were kept on hand. Can you employ any persons to collect information to be relied on, in the chief potato-growing districts in Ireland? Would a person of intelligence specially sent to Galway, Cork, etc., have better means of ascertaining the facts and the prospects of the failure than can be derived from written reports from stipendiary magistrates or others? I need not recommend to you the utmost reserve as to the future, I mean as to the possibility of government interference. There would be none without summoning parliament to adopt measures or confirm those of the executive.

(Lord Mahon and Edward Cardwell, *Memoirs by the Right Honourable Sir Robert Peel* (London, 1856–8), II–III, pp. 121–3)

Lord Heytesbury's reply to Sir Robert Peel.

Vice Regal Lodge, 17 October

My Dear Sir Robert,

I have to acknowledge yours of the 15th, which I have communicated most confidentially to Sir Thomas Fremantle [Secretary at War]. We are fully impressed with the immense importance of the question, and the consequences to which it may lead. Our attention has been earnestly directed to it, ever since the reports from the provinces have been so unsatisfactory. These reports continue to be of a very alarming nature, and leave no doubt upon the mind but that the potato crops have failed almost everywhere. I enclose an abstract from those received yesterday. A more favourable account indeed has been received by Mr A'Court [Private Secretary] from the Dean of Ossory [Revd. Charles Vignoles], whose letter I also enclose, but I must observe that the Dean, though a sensible, is a somewhat sanguine man, and is apt to view matters in the most favourable light. I am not inclined to think that a special commission would be able to collect more accurate information than that which is furnished by the several county inspectors. When the potato digging is a little more advanced, we might move the lieutenants of counties to call meetings of the resident landholders, with a view to ascertaining the amount of the evil, and their opinion of the measures most proper to be adopted ... Even if the crops would turn out to be as bad as is now apprehended, it is not thought that there will be any immediate pressure in the market. There will be enough saved for immediate consumption. The evil will probably be felt in all its intensity till towards the month of February, or beginning of spring. I am assured that there is no stock whatever of last year's potatoes in the country. Gloomy as all this is, it would be hardly prudent to adopt any very strong or decisive measures till the final result of the potato harvest can be fully ascertained. The digging will not be all over till about the second week in November.

I may refer you for what was done upon a former occasion to various proclamations of Lord Cornwallis in the years 1800–1, and to Acts, 41 George III, chapter 36, renewed by 43 George III, chapter 13. These acts are no longer in force, having only been passed to meet the difficulties then existing. [The acts prohibited the exportation of corn, potatoes and provisions from Ireland.]

(Mahon and Cardwell, *Memoirs by the Right Honourable Sir Robert Peel*, II–III, pp. 123–5)

Letter of 22 October 1845 from Sir Robert Peel to Sir James Graham, Home Secretary 1841–6.

... Lord Heytesbury, from his occasional remarks on proclamations, seems to labour under an impression that there is a constitutional right to issue them. Now there is absolutely none. There is no more abstract right to prohibit the export of a potato than to command any other violation of law. Governments have assumed, and will assume, in extreme cases, unconstitutional power, and will trust to the good sense of the people, convinced by the necessity to obey the proclamation, and to parliament to indemnify the issuers. The proclamations to which Lord Heytesbury refers, may be useful as precedents, but they leave the matter where they found it in point of law; they give no sort of authority. I have a strong impression that we shall do more harm than good by controlling the free action of the people in respect to the general export of these commodities, or the legal use of them ...

(O'Rourke, *History*, p. 83)

Extract from Sir Robert Peel's speech to the House of Commons in February 1846 on the need to repeal the Corn Laws, in which he argued that the removal of protective duties was imperative to enable the state charity compelled by the Irish crisis.

... When you are again exhorting a suffering people to fortitude under their privations, when you are telling them, 'These are the chastenings of an all-wise and merciful Providence, sent for some inscrutable but just and beneficent purpose – it may be, to humble our pride, or to punish our unfaithfulness, or to impress us with the sense of our own nothingness and dependence on His mercy'; when you are thus addressing your suffering fellow subjects, and encouraging them to bear without repining the dispensations of Providence, may God grant that by your decision of this night you may have laid in store for yourselves the consolation of reflecting that such calamities are, in truth, the dispensations of Providence – that they have not been caused, they have not been aggravated by laws of man restricting, in the hour of scarcity, the supply of food! ...

I wish it were possible to take advantage of this calamity for introducing among the people of Ireland the taste for a better and more certain provision for their support, than that which they have heretofore cultivated; and thereby diminishing the chances to which they will be constantly, I am afraid, liable, of recurrences of this great and mysterious visitation, by making potatoes the ordinary food of millions of our fellow subjects ...

(*Hansard*, House of Commons (16 February 1846))

In February 1846 a coercive Protection of Life Bill was introduced by the government. In the House of Lords in April, Peel argued that it would act as a deterrent to agrarian crime until the crisis in the Irish land system could be remedied, but staunchly defended the principles of property.

... A great number of estates are wholly unprofitable to their normal owners, being in the hands, not of proprietors, but receivers; and it is impossible to contemplate the number of estates in this position, and their unfruitfulness either to the creditor or the proprietor, without being forcibly convinced of the absolute necessity of some change in the law. I entertain the strongest opinion that there is no country where the maintenance of the great principles of property is more important than in Ireland. I do not believe that you could hope to establish prosperity in any country, to afford encouragement to industry, to excite a desire to realise the fruits of labour, if you violated any of the great principles of property ...

(*Hansard*, House of Lords (27 April 1846))

Comment in Ireland on the public work schemes.

Although we are not on the verge of famine in Ireland, as Mr O'Connell has stated in the House of Commons, yet the fact that there will be scarcity in the summer months, owing to the progress of the potato taint, makes it necessary to consider how any deficiency in food may be supplied. Government, to their credit be it spoken, have not neglected necessary precautions at this emergency. Several bills, which will have the effect of giving employment to the people of Ireland, have been introduced into the House of Commons by Sir Thomas Fremantle, Chief Secretary for Ireland, and they have already made considerable progress in their respective stages.

The first is a bill for the extension of public works in Ireland. It authorizes the commissioners of public works to make additional grants to the extent of £50,000. Government have wisely adopted a suggestion made by the Land Commissioners, in their report, that money advanced for public works should be repaid within twenty years, instead of seven as before, and that the interest be 'such as may be agreed upon', not five per cent as before. This bill has passed the House of Commons. A second measure of the same useful kind is the Drainage Bill. By this, money will be lent for the purpose of facilitating river drainages. It will enable landlords to improve their estates and give increased employment to the people. The bill has been read a second time. A third measure is the Fisheries Bill. The object of it is to afford encouragement to the construction of small piers and harbours, calculated to extend the deep fisheries. It is proposed to expend £50,000 in five years upon such profitable works. The bill was read a first time on Monday.

These bills are so many steps in the right direction. They will tend to the improvement of the physical condition of the country. Such measures ought to stop the mouths of agitators; and the peasantry of Ireland are not so devoid of discrimination as not to perceive the difference between an English government which takes means to feed and clothe them, and those who despoil them of their hard-earned pence and shillings.

(*Downpatrick Recorder* (7 February 1846))

Petition addressed to the Lord Lieutenant of Ireland, Lord Heytesbury, by farm labourers in the parish of Killeeneen, County Galway, requesting Indian corn (maize) for their district.

To His Excellency, Lord Heytesbury, the Lord Lieutenant and Governor-General of Ireland.

The humble petition of the farm labourers resident in the parish of Killeeneen, Barony of Dunkellon and County of Galway

Sheweth

That the price of potatoes in the district is over five pence per stone. That a day's wages, without food and now in the busiest season, is eight pence.

That many of us have wives and families – the number in each family is placed opposite our names herento affixed: that a stone of potatoes is the allowance to daily support one man, that some of us having families require two stones, others require three stones daily. That manifestly our wages and with constant employment, would not enable us to feed ourselves and families: that our potatoes are nearly run out, with some of us already exhausted.

That year after year we see wages having a tendency to fall lower and lower: that from the abundance of labourers, the rate of wages is kept down, whilst the price of food rises from scarcity and other causes: That annually new mouths are added and fresh hands from boyhood are able to join us, increasing our numbers, – still the land, that is the source of our food, is the same in quantity.

That we feel our remedy is cheap food, so as to bring the price along side the rate of wages; because, if wages cannot keep up to the price of food, food should keep pace in price with the rate of wages, – for, wages is the measure of food to feed the labourer: if not, the labourer would be cut of his share of the fruits of the Earth.

That we have heard that Indian corn meal, from foreign parts, has been brought over to this country by the Government, and to be sold at such prices as would enable poor men (earning *free* wages and obliged to buy *protected* price food, and now encreased in price from the failure of the potato crop) to feed themselves and families: That we seek no charity, we only want to get enough food in exchange for all we can obtain by hard and honest labour: we ask our measure of food, that wages merely represents.

That we want no relief by Poor Laws – that the whole world beholds our distress, and yet these laws require (us) to prove our distress, ere aid be afforded, by submitting to imprisonment and separation from our wives and children; and where are the work houses to hold our numbers.

That we never before petitioned Government to look to us: that we do so now, because we are assured our necessities shall be cared for.

Petitioners humbly pray that Your Excellency may order that an immediate supply of Indian corn meal be sent to this district and sold to us at prices our wages can reach.

Craughwell
April 13th 1846

(NAI, DP D405/1846)

Letter of 15 September 1846 from James Conry to T.N. Reddington of Castlebar, County Mayo.

... Undue and exorbitant prices have been demanded and paid in the provision markets of this town and in other markets of this country. Oatmeal which had up to a very late period been selling here at 14s. per cwt has within the last two weekly markets here risen to the exorbitant price of 18s. 6d. per cwt, placing it almost beyond the reach of the great bulk of the population ... Flour and meal of every description have risen proportionately in price and this too at a time when all employment, either upon public works or from farming operations, has ceased. The people have therefore of necessity been compelled in increased numbers to resort to the government depot here for Indian meal to support existence. Up to yesterday this meal was supplied (in quantities not exceeding 7lbs for each applicant) at the rate of 10s. per cwt or 1s. 3d. per stone, an advance in one day of 20% ... Indian meal is issued here through a small window about two feet square, attended by only one person and the consequence is that many of the unfortunate parents of young and weak families are kept waiting amongst a crowd outside this window, consisting of hundreds of persons, for one, two or three hours before they can obtain a miserable pittance of meal to keep alive their wretched offspring and, as if to aggravate the evil, this store is not opened until the hour of ten o'clock in the morning and it is closed for the day at the hour of five in the afternoon ...

(NAI, DP 4899; Liam Swords, *In Their Own Words: The Famine in North Connacht* (Dublin, 1999), p. 71)

Instructions issued by the Relief Commission for use of Indian meal, early 1847.

INDIAN MEAL

As it is important to pursue the most economical mode of using Indian Meal, the following receipt for cooking it into porridge, which has been in use for some time in an extensive establishment, may be useful: –

RECEIPT

In five pints of boiling water mix one pound of Indian Meal, which afterwards boil for half an hour, on the evening previous to the porridge being required. The following morning, add a little hot water, and when it comes to a boil, let it boil slowly for at least half an hour.

If a larger quantity be made, it must be boiled for a longer time both in the evening and morning.

The weight will be increased six-fold ; that is to say, seven pounds of Indian Meal will produce at least forty-two pounds of substantial porridge.

The salt should not be added until near the time for using it.

It is important to mention that an increase of quantity is found to take place in the cookery of Indian Meal porridge, by the above mode of boiling it twice; that is, once over night, and again when giving it out the following morning. A party who has adopted this plan, states that an increase of one-fifth is thus effected; that the porridge appears to be quite as substantial; and that the boiling previous to its being cooked for use, gets rid of much of the raw taste which has been objected to.

(NAI, M 3486)

Sir Charles Trevelyan, Assistant Secretary to the Treasury, was mainly responsible for the administration of relief measures during the famine. A capable and strong character, he was rigid in regard to Treasury rules and regulations, developing policies to economise on Treasury expenditure during the famine. He held a severe conviction that the Irish famine was divinely ordained, and during it an evangelical providentialism was strongly evident in his words and actions.

Trevelyan's Views on the Potato Economy

A population, whose ordinary food is wheat and beef, and whose ordinary drink is porter and ale, can retrench in periods of scarcity, and resort to cheaper kinds of food, such as barley, oats, rice, and potatoes. But those who are habitually and entirely fed on potatoes live upon the extreme verge of human subsistence, and when they are deprived of their accustomed food, there is nothing cheaper to which they can resort. They have already reached the lowest point in the descending scale, and there is nothing beyond but starvation or beggary. Several circumstances aggravate the hazard of this position. The produce of the potato is more precarious than that of wheat or any other grain. Besides many other proofs of the uncertainty of this crop, there is no instance on record of any such failure of the crops of corn, as occurred in the case of the potatoes in 1821, 1845, 1846, and 1847, showing that this root can no longer be depended upon as a staple article of human food.

The potato cannot be stored so that the scarcity of one year may be alleviated by bringing forward the reserves of former years, as is always done in cornfeeding countries. Every year is thus left to provide subsistence for itself. When the crop is luxuriant, the surplus must be given to the pigs; and when it is deficient, famine and disease necessarily prevail. Lastly, the bulk of potatoes is such, that they can with difficulty be conveyed from place to place to supply local deficiencies, and it has often happened that severe scarcity has prevailed in districts within fifty miles of which potatoes were to be had in abundance. If a man use two pounds of meal a day (which is twice the amount of the ration found to be sufficient during the late relief operations), a hundredweight of meal will last him for fifty-six days; whereas a hundredweight of potatoes will not last more than eight days; and when it was proposed to provide seed potatoes for those who had lost their stock in the failure of 1845–46, the plan was found impracticable, because nearly a ton an acre would have been required for the purpose.

The potato does not, in fact, last even a single year. The old crop becomes unfit for use in July, and the new crop, as raised by the inferior husbandry of the poor, does not come into consumption until September; hence, July and August are called the 'meal months', from the necessity the people are under of living upon meal at that period. This is always a season of great distress and trial for the poorer peasants; and in the districts in which the potato system has been carried to the greatest extent, as, for instance, in the barony of Erris in the county of Mayo, there has been an annual dearth in the summer months for many years past. Every now and then a 'meal year' occurs, and the masses of the population become a prey to famine and fever, except so far as they may be relieved by charity.

In 1739, an early and severe frost destroyed the potatoes in the ground, and the helplessness and despair of the people having led to a great falling off of tillage in 1740, the calamity was prolonged to the ensuing year, 1741, which was long known as the *bliadhain an air*, or year of slaughter. The ordinary burial-grounds were not large enough to contain those who died by the roadside, or who were taken from the deserted cabins. The 'bloody flux' [bacillary dysentery] and 'malignant fever', having begun among the poor, spread to the rich, and numerous individuals occupying prominent positions in society, including one of the judges, Mr Baron Wainwright, and the Mayor of Limerick, Joseph Roche, Esq., and many others of the corporation, fell victims. Measures were adopted at Dublin on the principle of the English Poor Law, some of the most essential provisions of which appear to have been well understood in the great towns of Ireland in that day: and it was 'hoped, since such provision is made for the poor, the inhabitants of the city will discourage all vagrant beggars, and give their assistance that they may be sent to bridewell to hard labour, and thereby free themselves from a set of idlers who are a scandal and a reproach to the nation'. Soup kitchens and other modes of relief were established in different parts of the country, in which Primate Boulter and the Society of Friends took the lead; and numerous cargoes of corn were procured on mercantile account from the North American Colonies, the arrival of which was looked for with great anxiety. In only one point is there any decided difference between what took place in Ireland and the painful events which have just occurred, after a lapse of upwards of a century. The famine of 1741 was not regarded with any active interest in England or in any foreign country, and the subject is scarcely alluded to in the literature of the day. No measures were adopted either by the executive or the legislature for the purpose of relieving the distress caused by this famine. There is no mention of grants or loans; but an act was passed by the Irish parliament in 1741 (15 George II, chapter 8), 'For the more effectual securing the payment of rents, and preventing frauds by tenants'.

(C.E. Trevelyan, *The Irish Crisis* (London, 1848), pp. 9–13; Noel Kissane, *The Irish Famine: A Documentary History* (Dublin, 1995), pp. 18–19)

Letter from Sir Charles Trevelyan to Sir Randolph Routh, the head of the Army Commissariat Department and one of the Relief Commissioners.

Treasury, 3 February 1846

I feel satisfied that you will concentrate your whole energies on the direct and practical measures for the relief of the suffering to be anticipated from the impending scarcity. Whether we regard the possible extent of that suffering, the suddenness with which it may come upon us in various points, or the fearful consequences of its not being promptly relieved, the subject is one which calls for all our foresight and power of arrangement.

That indirect permanent advantages will accrue to Ireland from the scarcity and the measures taken for its relief, I entertain no doubt; but if we were to pursue these incidental objects to the neglect of any of the precautions immediately required to save the people from actual starvation, our responsibility would be fearful indeed. Besides, the greatest improvement of all which could take place in Ireland would be to teach the people to depend upon themselves for developing the resources of their country, instead of having recourse to the assistance of the government on every occasion. Much has been done of late years to put this important matter on its proper footing; but if a firm stand is not made against the prevailing disposition to take advantage of this crisis to break down all barriers, the true permanent interest of the country will, I am convinced suffer in a manner which will be irreparable in our time.

Up to the present date, nothing has, so far as I am aware, been done which should prevent a perfectly sound line from being taken, and one which will bear looking back upon, after the excitement arising from present circumstances shall have passed away.

(Kissane, *The Irish Famine*, p. 50)

Letter from Trevelyan to Lord Monteagle, a County Limerick landlord, who had served as Chancellor of the Exchequer from 1835 to 1839 and was on the 'moderate liberal' wing of the Whig Party.

To the Right Hon. Lord Monteagle.

My Dear Lord.

I have had the pleasure of receiving your letter dated 1st instant, and before proceeding to the subjects more particularly treated in it, I must beg of you to dismiss all doubt from your mind of the magnitude of the existing calamity and its danger not being fully known and appreciated in Downing Street.

The government establishments are strained to the utmost to alleviate this great calamity and avert this danger, as far as it is in the power of government to do so; and in the whole course of my public service, I never witnessed such entire self-devotion and such hearty and cordial co-operation on the part of officers belonging to different departments met together from different parts of the world, as I have on this occasion. My purchases are carried to the utmost point short of transferring the famine from Ireland to England and giving rise to a counter popular pressure here, which it would be more difficult to resist because it would be founded on strong considerations of justice.

But I need not remind your lordship that the ability even of the most powerful government is extremely limited in dealing with a social evil of this description. It forms no part of the functions of government to provide supplies of food or to increase the productive powers of the land. In the great institution of the business of society, it falls to the share of government to protect the merchant and the agriculturist in the free exercise of their respective employments, but not itself to carry on those employments; and the condition of a community depends upon the result of the efforts which each member of it makes in his private and individual capacity ...

In Ireland the habit has proverbially been to follow a precisely opposite course, and the events of the last six weeks furnish a remarkable illustration of what I do not hesitate to call this defective part of the national character. The nobility and gentry have met in their respective baronies, and beyond making the presentments required by law, they have, with rare exceptions, confined themselves to memorials and deputations calling upon the government to do everything, as if they have themselves no part to perform in this great crisis of the country. The government is expected to open shops for the sale of food in every part of Ireland, to make all the railroads in Ireland, and to drain and improve the whole of the land of Ireland, to the extent of superseding the proprietor in the management of his own estate, and arranging with his tenants the terms on which the rent etc. is to be adjusted ...

I must give expression to my feelings by saying that I think I see a bright light shining in the distance through the dark cloud which at present hangs over Ireland. A remedy has been already applied to that portion of the maladies of Ireland which was traceable to political causes ... The deep and inveterate root of Social evil remained, and I hope I am not guilty of irreverence in thinking that, this being altogether beyond the power of man, the cure has been applied by the direct stroke of an all wise Providence in a manner as unexpected and unthought of as it is likely to be effectual. God grant that we may rightly perform our part and not turn into a curse what was intended for a blessing. The ministers of religion and especially the pastors of the Roman Catholic Church, who possess the largest share of influence over the people of Ireland, have well performed their part; and although few indications appear from any proceedings which have yet to come before the public that the landed proprietors have even taken the first step of preparing for the conversion of the land now laid down to potatoes to grain cultivation, I do not despair of seeing this class in society still taking the lead which their position requires of them, and preventing the social revolution from being so extensive as it otherwise must become.
Believe me, my dear lord, yours very sincerely,
C.E. Trevelyan
Treasury, 9 October 1846

(NLI, Ms 13,397, Monteagle Papers)

During previous famines public works had been offered as a solution to the prevailing distress. The Board of Works was established by an act of parliament in 1831 entitled an Act for the Extension and Promotion of Public Works in Ireland. Early in 1846, the British Cabinet decided that public works should be jointly financed by treasury grants and local taxation. Employment was given to those with relief tickets from local relief committees. Late in the spring of 1846 road works and drainage schemes commenced in most Irish counties. Many obstacles arose regarding the nature and quality of the work performed on relief schemes and in controlling the huge number of labourers involved. The reports of county inspecting officers, originally appointed by the Relief Commission to co-ordinate the relief work of local committees, contained many observations on the operations of public works and the difficulties encountered by those wishing to fish.

Peel retired from office in June 1846, to be replaced by the Whig Lord John Russell, who remained Prime Minister until 1852 and was assumed to be relatively sympathetic to Ireland. Preoccupied with the debate about land reform, he was ultimately hindered by previous patterns of Irish famines, which had rarely lasted more than a year, and an affiliation to a free trade ideology which was seen in itself as a solution to the famine crisis, particularly by those who believed that state intervention would only encourage famine victims to do nothing for themselves. Thus the government would neither countenance the importation of cheap foodstuffs nor prevent the export of food. However, Russell's authority at Cabinet level was undermined by numerous forces which pushed him in contradictory directions, as he presided over a political party containing a number of different factions.

Speaking in the House of Lords, Earl Grey, son of the second Earl Grey (who had served as Prime Minister from 1830 to 1834) gave his assessment of the state of Ireland. Grey went on to serve as Colonial Secretary from 1846 to 1852. A religious radical who attacked the position of the established Church in Ireland, Grey believed in using Poor Law reform as a mechanism for enforcing moral improvement and belonged to the 'moralist liberal' wing of the party. Like others on this wing of the party, he asserted that the abolition of economic protection would create a moral imperative in people to act in a progressive manner to improve their own and others' welfare.

The state of Ireland is one which is notorious. We know the ordinary condition of that country to be one both of lawlessness and wretchedness. It is so described by every competent authority. There is not an intelligent foreigner coming to our shores, who turns his attention to the state of Ireland, but who bears back with him such a description. Ireland is the one weak place in the solid fabric of British power; Ireland is the one deep (I had almost said ineffaceable) blot upon the brightness of British honour. Ireland is our disgrace. It is the reproach, the standing disgrace, of this country that Ireland remains in the condition she is. It is so regarded throughout the whole civilised world. To ourselves we may palliate it if we will, and disguise the truth; but we cannot conceal it from others. There is not, as I have said, a foreigner – no matter whence he comes, be it from France, Russia, Germany, or America – there is no native of any foreign country, different as their forms of government may be, who visits Ireland, and who on his return does not congratulate himself that he sees nothing comparable with the condition of that country at home.

If such be the state of things, how then does it arise and what is its cause? My Lords, it is only by misgovernment that such evils could have been produced; the mere fact that Ireland is in so deplorable and wretched a condition saves whole volumes of argument, and is of itself a complete and irrefutable proof of the misgovernment to which she has been subjected. Nor can we lay to our souls the 'flattering unction' that this misgovernment was only of ancient date, and has not been our doing. It is not enough in our own excuse to say, 'No wonder this state of things exists; the government of Ireland before the union was the most ingeniously bad that was ever contrived in the face of the world; it was the government of a corrupt minority, sustained by the superior power of this great country in oppressing and tyrannizing over the great body of the nation; such a system of government could not fail to leave behind it a train of fearful evils from which we are still suffering to the present day.'

To a certain extent, no doubt, this is true. No man has a stronger opinion than I regarding the iniquitous system of misgovernment in Ireland prior to the Union. But the Union is not an event of yesterday. It is nearly half a century since that measure passed. For nearly fifty years, now, Ireland has been under the immediate control of the Imperial Parliament. Since it has been so, a whole generation has grown up, and is now passing away to be replaced by another; and in that time, I ask you, what impression has been made upon the evils of Ireland? It is true some good has been done. I gladly acknowledge that many useful measures have been adopted, which have, I hope, contributed in some respects to the improvement of Ireland; but none of these measures have gone to the root of the social disease to which Ireland is prey, in the worst symptoms of which no amelioration whatever can be observed; the wretchedness and misery of the population have experienced no abatement. Upon that point I can quote high authority. I find that the Commission presided over by a noble Earl, whom I do not now see in his place [the Earl of Devon], reported the year before last, that 'improvement was indeed beginning to take place in agriculture, but there had been no corresponding advance in the condition and comforts of the labouring classes'. By the report of that commission we are informed that the agricultural labourers are still suffering the greatest privations and hardships, and still depend upon casual and precarious employment for their subsistence; that they are badly fed, badly clothed, badly housed, and badly paid for their labour; and the commissioners conclude this part of their report by saying: 'We cannot forbear expressing our strong sense of the patient endurance which the labouring classes have generally exhibited under sufferings greater, we believe, than the people of any other country have ever endured.'

But there is another symptom of the condition of Ireland, which seems to me even more alarming than the prevalence of distress – I mean the general alienation of the whole mass of the nation from the institutions under which they live, and the existence in their minds of a strong deep feeling of hostility to the form of government under which they are placed. This feeling, which is the worst feature in the case, seems to be rather gaining strength than to be diminishing. I am led to that opinion by what I heard two years ago fall from the Secretary of State for the Home Department [Sir James Graham] in the House of Commons. I heard that Right Hon. Gentleman, in answer to a speech made by a noble friend of mine, distinctly admit that we had military occupation of Ireland, but that in no other sense could it be said to be governed; that it was occupied by troops, not governed like England. Such was the admission of the Secretary of State for the Home Development.

(*Hansard*, House of Lords (23 March 1846), pp. 1345–7; Kissane, *The Irish Famine*, pp. 10–11)

Speech made by Lord John Russell to the House of Commons in August 1846 on the Irish situation.

Having already stated the evils which have in practice arisen from interference by the government with the supply of the public food, I have only to add that we do not propose to interfere with the regular mode by which Indian corn and other kinds of grain may be brought into the country. We propose to leave that trade as much at liberty as possible. But there may be particular cases, as there were in 1836 and 1839, where, in consequence of the part of the country where the famine prevailed being very inaccessible, it became necessary to employ the commissariat officers. As a general rule, however, we shall still take care not to interfere with the regular operations of merchants for the supply of food to the country, or with the retail trade, which was much deranged by the operations of last year. With regard to relief committees, we propose that they should for a time be constituted, taking care to avoid those errors which have hitherto ensued from want of experience, and guided by the lights we have received from the practice as hitherto established. In particular, we shall endeavour to avoid the giving of tickets, by members of relief committees, to persons who are not in need of relief ...

Sir, as I stated at the commencement, this is a special case, requiring the intervention of parliament. I consider that the circumstances I have stated, of that kind of food which constitutes the subsistence of millions of people in Ireland being subjected to the dreadful ravages of this disease, constitute this a case of exception, and render it imperative on the government and the parliament to take extraordinary measures for relief. I trust that the course I propose to pursue will not be without its counterbalancing advantages; that it will show the poorest among the Irish people that we are not insensible, here, to the claims which they have on us as the parliament of the United Kingdom; that the whole credit of the Treasury and means of the country are ready to be used as it is our burden duty to use them, and will, whenever they can be usefully applied, be so disposed as to avert famine and to maintain the people of Ireland; and that we are now disposed to take advantage of the unfortunate spread of this disease among the potatoes to establish public works which may be of permanent utility. I trust, Sir, that the present state of things will have that counterbalancing advantage in the midst of many misfortunes and evil consequences. I know that I need not detain you any longer than to assure the committee and the House that we consider that our predecessors in office did show a very laudable anxiety to meet the evil – that the remedies they applied were suited to the occasion – that we shall endeavour to imitate the spirit in which they acted, while we shall endeavour to take advantage of their experience to correct errors which were inevitable in consequence of such unforseen difficulties ...

(Hansard, House of Commons (17 August 1846))

Before the full impact of the famine was apparent, Russell was not averse to using language critical of Irish landlords and the operation of the land system, and even contemplated some form of dual ownership based on the rights enjoyed by Ulster tenants. Ultimately, however, Russell's cabinet was divided on these issues, and the famine frustrated any planned Whig reform programmes in Ireland. The suggestions for reform were not to be proffered again until William Gladstone pursued the matter in the late 1860s.

Letter of April 1846 from Russell to Lord Bessborough, Lord Lieutenant of Ireland, 1846–7, April 1846.

My objection is that the law allows [the landlord] to do such an act as this. In England public opinion would prevent his doing it, but I am sorry to say that powerful engine is wanting in Ireland both in respect to this and many other cases in which the poorest classes of person are concerned. This must be altered somehow or other before Ireland can be quiet ... As it is all the laws affecting the poor appear to have been framed for the protection of the rich.

(Cited in Peter Gray, *Famine, Land and Politics: British Government and Irish Society* (Dublin, 1999), p. 142)

Letter of November 1847 from Russell to Lord Clarendon, Lord Lieutenant of Ireland 1847–52, November 1847.

I have always thought the tenant-right of Ulster took part of the property of the landlord to give to the tenant – But I imagine the result is that the landlord gets more rent, and is less shot at than the landlord of Tipperary – In Prussia there was a far more violent interference with property and the country has flourished since – In fact many landlords in Ireland allow it for the sake of peace ...

It is quite true that landlords in England would not bear to be shot like hares or partridges by miscreants banded for murderous purposes. But neither does any landlord in England turn out fifty persons at once, and burn their homes over their heads, giving them no provision for the future. The murders are atrocious, but so are the ejectments. The truth is that a civil war between landlords and tenants has been raging for 80 years, marked by barbarity on both sides. I am willing to finish the contest, if it can be finished by leaving the law to its operation, by the gradual influence of civilization, by introducing and fostering education. But if stringent laws are required, they must bear on both sides in the contest ...

(Cited in Gray, *Famine, Land and Politics*, p. 184)

Letter from Trevelyan to Richard Pennefather, Under Secretary, concerning public works.

Treasury Chambers, 26 June 1846

Sir,

With reference to their Lordships' minute dated 16th instant, on the third monthly report of the Commissioners of Public Works, a copy of which was forwarded to you with my letter of the same date, I am commanded by the Lord Commissioners of Her Majesty's Treasury to state that, having reason to believe that numerous persons who do not really stand in need of relief are employed on the works which have been sanctioned under the Act, 9 Victoria, chapter 1 [March 1846], for the relief of the people suffering from scarcity, and the rates of wages are given exceeding what is required for providing subsistence for the workpeople and their families, and holding out a temptation to engage in the works carried on under the above mentioned act in preference to other means of employment which are open to them, their Lordships request that you will suggest to the Lord Lieutenant that the Board of Works and the Relief Commission should be directed to issue such instructions to the superintendents of the works and to the local relief committees, as will secure a due observance of the rules which have been laid down for the proper administration of the funds provided for the relief of the people suffering from the late failure of the potato crop in Ireland.

I am, etc.,

C.E. Trevelyan

(BBP (6), *Relief of Distress, Board of Works*, pp. 94–5)

Letter from General Inglis, Assistant Commissary General, reporting to the Board of Public Works regarding regional disturbances.

Enclosure.
Lieutenant Inglis to Mr Walker.

Bruff, September 29, 1846

I beg to submit, for the information of the Board, the following description of the proceedings at the Extraordinary Presentment Sessions, held yesterday, at Kilfinan, for the Barony of Coshlea, under 9 and 10 Vic., chap. 107. The County Surveyor, Mr Kearney, having prepared statements showing the extra amounts remaining in hand of the several grants for the district, proceeded to lay the information contained in them before the magistrates and cess [rate] payers assembled. He next gave statements showing the amounts required to complete the works for which the original grants have proved insufficient, amounting in all to £3470 15s. And all were approved, not however without some very vehement discussion. He next commenced a list of about 20 works, consisting chiefly of new lines, several hills cutting and dykes filling, all of which, after some deliberation, were approved. The total amount required for these works being about £9186. It was then remarked by some that a certain portion of the eastern side of the barony had been neglected. Most violent language was made use of by certain gentlemen on the bench; they refused to hear the applications for works in the neglected district, which Mr Kearney heard were to be brought forward by other persons; the greatest confusion ensued, the excitement extended to the mob in the Court-house, and from it to a very large mob outside, and from this time forward all was riot and confusion. This disturbance appeared to be the signal for indiscriminately throwing in applications for works of all description. Sums were named without any regard whatever to the nature or extent of the work. Works proposed without knowing or even caring about the most advantageous plan of executing them. Everything was approved. In fact, it appeared that nobody dared oppose.

During this the riot both outside and inside the Court became more and more violent, and the confusion on the bench, more and more confused; and at length we left the house and passed, with some difficulty, through the crowd to a neighbouring hotel. Such has been the result of a meeting convened to provide means for the relief of, and consequently measures for the establishment of peace and quiet amongst the population of the most extensive barony in this division of the county; and I am of opinion that this result cannot be viewed in too serious a light. It has opened our proceedings for the ensuing year with riot and disorder, and it would be unreasonable to expect in the natural course that this disorder would give place to tranquillity and peace, or that the excitement that has now been aroused in the minds of the people will readily be allayed; and unless allayed, anything approaching to system must be upset; and without a perfect system our proceedings must terminate in a failure.

I do not for a moment hesitate to state that all I have mentioned above, is entirely to be attributed to the intemperate language made use of by some of the members of the Court. But, for the inconsiderate behaviour of these persons, I thoroughly believe the proceedings would have terminated as they commenced, namely, in regularity and quiet; and I regret the more to believe that such is the case, for I see clearly how little assistance may be expected from those residing in this district, in carrying out the difficult task now before us.

(BBP (6), *Relief of Distress, Board of Works*, pp. 94–5)

The following proclamation was issued by Henry Labouchere, Chief Secretary for Ireland 1846–7 and later President of the Board of Trade.

Proclamation

Dublin Castle, October 2, 1846

Whereas it has been represented to the Lord Lieutenant, that in various parts of the country numerous assemblages of people have committed acts of violence, by attacking the shops of the bakers and the stores of merchants, and by interrupting the free traffic in provisions, and otherwise disturbing the public peace:

His Excellency is determined, by every means in his power, to protect the lawful trade in the articles of food, the complete security of which is essential to the subsistence of the people; and he earnestly warns all persons of the dangers which they incur by taking part in these illegal proceedings.

The Lord Lieutenant has also been informed that a disposition has, in some instances, been manifested by the labourers employed in Public Works to resist the arrangements which the officers of the Board of Works have made, in order to ensure their proper execution, by task or piece-work, as well as to endeavour, by violence, to obtain a higher rate of wages. These officers are acting under the express directions of the Government, and if this improper interference is persevered in, the Lord Lieutenant will be compelled to order the works to be discontinued.

The Lord Lieutenant confidently relies on the continued support of magistrates and others of station and influence, in his efforts to maintain tranquillity, as well as to mitigate the effects of the calamity with which it has pleased Divine Providence to afflict this country; and he desires, in an especial manner, to thank the ministers of religion, of all persuasions, for their useful and exemplary conduct on this trying occasion.

By His Excellency's command,

H. LABOUCHERE

(BBP (6) *Relief of Distress, Board of Works*, p. 67)

Friar Theobald Mathew was a Capuchin monk who became famed for his relentless temperance crusade in Ireland, which was inaugurated through the Cork Total Abstinence Society in 1838 and quickly spread to the rest of the country. Initially an attempt to address the serious issue of excessive drinking, it soon became a populist crusade based around the idea of en masse pledging. It was a phenomenal short-term success, but declined within a decade and left no durable structures behind. Undoubtedly the famine and its associated social disruption, emigration and death fatally undermined the temperance movement. Mathew combined his temperance work with famine relief endeavours, and took on the role of unofficial, but highly respected, adviser to the authorities on Irish affairs. Frequently speaking out against the increases in food prices, he castigated the profits corn and flour traders were making. Friar Mathew served on the Relief Committee for Cork city, and for a time turned his own home into a soup kitchen. As conditions worsened he concentrated his entire efforts on relief work. He wrote the following letter to Trevelyan from Cork on 20 November 1846.

... Concluding that you now enjoy a little relaxation of your excessive labours, I presume to address you on a subject of, in my estimation, the highest importance. I am not called upon to give an opinion as to the utility of the Public Works now in progress; necessity gave them birth, and they must be executed; but it afflicted me deeply to find the benevolent intentions of Government frustrated, and the money, so abundantly distributed, made a source of demoralization and intemperance. Wherever these Presentment Works are commenced, public houses are immediately opened, the magistrates, with a culpable facility, granting licences.

The overseers and pay-clerks generally hold their offices in these pestiferous erections; even some of these officers have a pecuniary interest in these establishments. It often happens that the entire body of labourers, after receiving payment, instead of buying provisions for their famishing families, consume the greater part in the purchase of intoxicating drink. The same deplorable abuse takes place on the different railway lines. It would be far better to have the pay clerks, who travel in cars, bring with them writing-desks, and pay the men at the different work stations, than to congregate them in the evenings at these public houses. These establishments are not necessary in Ireland, for our labourers do not eat in such places; they only drink to get drunk. I do not make a complaint of any of the

Officers of the Board of Works; I only place before you the painful result of my late observations ... I am, I confess, puzzled by the uncertainty of what will be the employment of the people next season. If the cultivation of flax was as general in the west as it is in the North, there would be sufficient remunerative labour for all, males and females. Belfast market would at present purchase all that could be prepared in the south and west. I am co-operating, might and main, with the Belfast Flax Association. The progress we are making in Munster is very slow, the poverty of the people preventing them from buying flax-seed, or inducing them to buy an inferior kind. Instead of the fine Dutch seed, they buy Russian or American ...

Trevelyan passed on the letter to Lieutenant-Colonel Jones, Chairman of the Board of Works, who replied as follows to Trevelyan on 26 November 1846

... The subject of Father Mathew's communication to you is, I am afraid, too true, in one respect, as regards the effects produced by the abundance which now prevails among the labouring classes. I have heard several complaints as regards the increase of drunkenness. As to the payments being made in public-houses, that is directly opposed to our regulations; but to prevent irregularities of that sort is very difficult. The establishing of shebeen or drinking houses or huts adjacent to the works is not within our power to prevent, and in general is a concomitant with all public works. We do our best to correct abuses and irregularities immediately we hear of them ...

(BPP (6) *Relief of Distress, Board of Works*, pp. 271–3)

William Bishop was a County Inspecting Officer for the Relief Commission with responsibility for Cork. The following extracts are from two reports he sent to Sir Randolph Routh.

5th December 1846, Cork City

The same class of grain crops produced last year are now in progress, but not to a greater extent. More turnips are being sown, than was last year – grain is fast disappearing – much of the grain sold last year in Cork was sold by country people and taken there. Home produce will now be consumed, since demand on committees for Indian Meal is limited – a good description sold last week in Cork was sold here for the same price as in Dublin. 31,000 pigs sold in Cork this year – last year 5780. Bread stuffs consumed in Cork and vicinity daily 100 tons – the merchants have not more than 4,000 tons in store. Delivery of wheat small, farms having used much of it themselves. Large deliveries of barley and oats becoming scarce – Oatmeal £21 million, Indian Meal £18 per ton. The deposits made this year in the Cork Savings Bank are less than those of the preceding years. In Oct. and Nov. '45 the deposits were £21,059, in the same time this year only £19,032 ... Conacre has nearly disappeared in these parts. The people do not adapt themselves to their altered condition – nor do they make any effort to supply a new class of food to procure future subsistence. They take Public Works as an immediate source of relief and throw themselves on them – even if they were disposed to cultivate their pieces of ground, they have not means of subsistence whilst doing so. The lands abandoned by the poorer classes remain uncultivated ...

(NAI RLFC 7/06/05)

31 January 1847

... Fishermen are in distress from two causes – they are half fishermen and half farmers; have suffered a total loss of potato crop and there is no remuneratory market for the fish. The fishing grounds off the south and south west coast are considered to abound with fish. Baltimore, recommended by Mr Barry, Inspector of Fisheries, as a station for a curing establishment, appears to be well situated for the purpose. It appears by the letter of Mr Barry that there is no longer any demand for the fish. He mentioned that the cured fish of last season were not bought by the usual travelling dealers called Jolters and had in consequence to be taken to Cork, where, however, so small a price was received that the fishermen incurred much loss and have since gone to the Public Works for subsistence. He also mentioned that within a fortnight preceding the date of his report (9th Jan '47), a fisherman near Baltimore brought in the produce of three nights fishing – 27 score of cod, Ling and Hake, which he offered at 2d and 1.5d each, but could not obtain buyers and then carted them to Skibbereen, where he received so little for them that after paying the cost of carriage he had not six pence for himself. He also, went to the Public Works. There is plainly at present, no market for fish in the south west of Cork and everywhere the demand for cured fish has declined.

(NAI, RLFC 7/06/32)

W. Millikin was the County Inspecting Officer with responsibility for Galway. He sent similar reports to Routh.

8 December, 1846

Proceeded to Clifden and examined the manner in which the duties of Mr C.C. Parker were conducted – his cash and the accounts were most creditably kept. Examined the balance of cash and the remains of supplies and they agree with his books – he is an excellent officer, he knows the wants of the people so well that his communications might seem as if he was advocating their cause, but he is fully aware of his duty to the government ... Between Galway and Clifden saw only two men at work on the land – at Oughterard about 300 men were at work on the road, waiting to be paid – these were nearly all farmers, or their sons – these will not work on their own land while they can find other employment – fewer paupers here than in some localities – the county about Connemara is thinly peopled – very little seed has been sown and scarcely any preparation for spring crops. The fisheries have not commenced at Roundstone or Clifden, herrings not having appeared on the coast – the fishing Depot will be most beneficial – the Fishermen are a different class of men – keep by themselves and have laws and customs of their own – they are a superior race compared with the other lower classes.

(NAI, RLFC 7/11/1–2)

7 February 1847

Visited the village of Spidall yesterday, on the western coast leading to Lettermore Island, to attend a meeting of the Spidall Relief Committee ... a discussion arose concerning a Blacksmith being struck off the works – his Landlord urging that although the man had a comfortable house, he had not business at his trade – it was stated that the barrow and [other] instruments used on the works were taken from Galway at a dearer rate than could be had from here – besides the advantage of employing the people taken from there, thus were the tradesmen obliged to seek relief from Public Works. The chair of the committee stated that he had handbarrows made for 2s. 6d. each which the contractor charged 4s. 6d. for – this was stated to Captain Hutchinson, Inspecting Officer of the Board of Works. Fisheries entirely neglected owing to the want of harbourage – along a coast of 25 miles there is only one safe harbour (Barna) – there is an old pier at Spidall – which a moderate sum would repair and it would be a good shelter – some time ago a gale overtook the boats; 57 got the shelter of this pier and 45 were lost – have ceased fishing altogether. They have often desired to have the evil remedied – it would increase the wealth of the country and employ many – the people are industrious and every spot, even amongst the rocks cultivated either with bere or barley ...

(NAI RLFC 7/11/2)

The following notice was issued by the Cavan Relief Committee in response to complaints received concerning abuses of public works schemes.

NOTICE

CAVAN RELIEF COMMITTEE

The Relief Committee have received numerous complaints of persons having obtained employment in the Public Works in this district, who do not come within the description laid down in the instructions issued by Government to the Relief Committees, that is 'persons who are destitute of means of support, or for whose support such employment is actually necessary'.

It is obvious that Pensioners at a shilling a day, Farmers (or their sons) possessing a cart and horse, and several cows, with stacks of oats in their haggard, cannot be included in this description; and yet many such, it is stated to the Committee, are at present employed.

When such persons once take into consideration that, as employment obviously cannot be afforded to all, their obtaining it throws out of the work poor destitute and starving people, the Committee confidently trust they will voluntarily withdraw and give up their tickets.

The Committee, however, will continue to receive complaints; and if the party complained of does not withdraw of his own accord, he will be called upon to shew upon what grounds he claims to be employed on the Public Works.

The Committee will not recommend for employment Servants or Labourers who are actually engaged, or those who leave their employers without consent.

When any Gentleman or Farmer requires Labourers, to be paid at the same rate adopted in the Public Works, if he will notify to the Committee the names of those he wishes to hire, they shall be immediately struck off their Lists so long as they are thus required; the Committee being authorised to afford employment to those alone who cannot obtain it elsewhere.

The Committee are informed that Carts and Horses belonging to wealthy farmers are employed at the Public Works. This they consider quite unjustifiable. There are persons holding little or no land, who keep a Cart and Horse entirely for hire, and actually live by it. Of such, a list might, without much difficulty, be made; and the Committee think that such might fairly obtain employment at the usual wages, of 2s. 6d. per day, under the Board of Works, provided they cannot procure it elsewhere. But if it shall be found necessary to employ the Carts of persons not in want, the Committee recommend that they shall receive three men from the Public Works in exchange, or if they prefer it, two men, and the wages of the third in cash; but that in no case, shall the wages of 2s. 6d. a day for a man, cart, and horse be paid, unless to those in the list before mentioned.

The Committee are of opinion that, for the future, Overseers and Check Clerks, as far as may be found practicable, should be selected from persons at present in the Public Works; their merit might be judged from their conduct while employed, and if any should be found deserving of promotion, it would be a great incentive to others, and would also be a saving of the Public Money.

FARNHAM
Chairman
November 10, 1846

(NAI, RLFC 3/2 Cavan)

Letter from J. E. Mennons, Secretary and Treasurer of a relief committee in Roscommon, to Sir Randolph Routh, describing conditions in his district.

Oran Cloonigormican & Donamon Parishes Relief Committee
Barony of Ballymoe, Co. Roscommon

Tempe Roscommon, 30 Jany. 1847

Sir,

In forwarding to you the annexed list of personal subscriptions collected by the Relief Committee, I have been directed to bring under your notice the extent of the destitution within the district.

The condition of the peasantry is of the most wretched description. Of the larger portion of them, the sole dependence was the potatoe crop which here was a complete failure having, in consequence of the heavy nature of the soil, been sown late and was therefore attacked by the disease at an early period of its growth before the root was at all formed. Within these few weeks two persons have died of starvation in this district and innumerable cases have come under the notice of the committee where death has been accelerated by an insufficiency of food.

Cases of sheep stealing and highway robbery, offences hitherto almost unknown in this district, are of hourly occurrence, nor do the numerous arrests or perpetrators of those offences seem in the slightest degree to deter others.

The district is unfortunately circumstanced in its means of receiving relief. The landlords of the destitute poor are, in almost every instance, absentees and from the proprietors of a large portion of the district no relief is likely to be received as their estates are under the control of the Court of Chancery. This is the case with the property of the Heirs of the Honourable Anthony Malone, Daniel H. Farrell, Lord Oranmore, Balfe's Minors, and Goff's Minors, which you will perceive by a glance at the accompanying list form a large portion of the district. Another circumstance which tends, in a great degree, to prevent us from receiving relief is the extent to which subletting has been carried [on] in the district and on properties [on] which are the largest proportion of paupers. The immediate landlords are generally not in a position to contribute and the head landlords consider that the tenants have no claim on them. In some cases persons of the poorest class have built huts on bog or other waste land and pay rent to no person.

The few resident gentry farm the greater portion of their own land and employ the few poor tenantry they have while they pay a large share of the taxation under the Relief Act, so that little can be expected from them.

Three public works are now in progress in this district but, as you will see from the return herewith sent, the number employed bears but a small proportion to those requiring relief, and that proportion is even less than would appear from the return as the committee have not registered any applicants at their last two meetings, not having any requisition for men, and being engaged revising their lists. The number of fresh applicants for employment in actual destitution would probably now amount to 100 more, and is every day increasing.

The average rate of wages for the last month does not exceed 7d. per day and, as each person employed has on average a family of 5 persons to support, each member will scarcely have 1.5d. per day, while oatmeal, their usual food, now sells at 27s. per cwt. To widows and infirm old men the public works can afford no relief, and they have not now the usual refuge for such persons, the poor house, as the guardians of the Roscommon Union, for which the district is a portion, have determined to admit no more paupers in consequence of the crowded state of the house.

I am Sir

Your Obedient Servant

J. E. Mennons

Secretary

(NAI, RLFC, II/2b 9837, Roscommon)

Abstract Return of the Number of Persons Employed in the Undermentioned Counties, for the Week Ending 29 August 1846

On Roads

Clare	16,524	Sligo	12,952
Cork	10,602	Tipperary	10,222
Cavan	1,247	Wicklow	324
Dublin	172	Waterford	520
Galway	40,355	Westmeath	139
King's	1,220	Total	196,645
Kerry	2,977		
Limerick	2,244	**On Drainage**	12,503
Leitrim	11,112		
Louth	447	Total	209,148
Meath	2,289		
Mayo	41,203	Shannon Union	750
Queen's	330		
Roscommon	41,766	Daily Average	34,858

Office of Public Works, 1 September 1846
(BBP (1), Relief of Distress, Board of Works, p. 17)

Return Showing the Daily Average Number of Persons Employed on Public Works in Ireland, for Week ending 14 November 1846

Leinster		Ulster	
Carlow	260	Antrim	-
Drogheda, Town of	-	Belfast Town	-
Dublin	50	Carrickfergus	-
Dublin, City of	-	Armagh	217
Kildare	384	Cavan	1,277
Kilkenny	1,031	Donegal	-
Kilkenny, City of	164	Fermanagh	1,369
King's County	1,018	Londonderry	-
Longford	4,762	Monagan	2,131
Louth	3,338	Tyrone	-
Meath	6,423		
Queen's County	829	Total	4,994
Westmeath	2,547		
Wexford	3,876		
Wicklow	188		
Total	24,870		

Munster		Connaught	
Clare	28,929	Galway	13,687
Cork	14,154	Leitrim	3,016
Cork, City of	170	Mayo	17,316
Kerry	12,792	Roscommon	34,131
Limerick	15,767	Sligo	8,942
Limerick, City of	643		
Tipperary	12,568	**Total**	77,092
Waterford	3,376		
Total	88,399		
Grand Total	195,355		

(BBP (6) *Relief of Distress, Board of Works*, p. 273)

Crimes Reported During the Great Famine (1844 = 100)

	1845	1846	1847	1848	1849	1850	1851
All Crime	128	196	332	223	236	168	145
Burglary	97	269	561	279	134	73	141
Robbery	124	257	559	588	460	409	319
Rape	89	92	31	52	34	65	43
Homicide	95	116	145	117	139	95	108
Cattle and sheep stealing	79	368	1223	821	993	585	448

(NAI *Return Of Outrages*. The data excludes the Dublin Metropolitan Area)

Reported Crimes, 1844–1847

	1845	1845	1847
Jan – Feb	1,236 (1108)	1,555 (1412)	5,082 (2246)
Mar – Apr	1,352 (1219)	1,500 (1351)	4,469 (1980)
May – June	1,617 (1531)	1,226 (1096)	4,208 (1904)
July – Aug	1,201 (1097)	956 (830)	1,551 (1029)
Sept –Oct	972 (892)	2,246 (1838)	1,640 (1283)
Nov – Dec	1,184 (1054)	4,327 (2258)	

(NAI T64/367A/3. The numbers in brackets exclude cattle stealing. Both cited in Cormac
O'Gráda, *Ireland: A New Economic History 1780–1939* (Oxford, 1994), p. 203)

Extracts from the Sixteenth Annual Report of the Commissioners of Public Works, 1848.

It would be improper to close our report for the year 1847 without some notice of the operations for 'relief' which it has devolved upon this board to execute ... In former years, seasons of partial distress have occurred in Ireland, and the local calamity by which large numbers of persons were suddenly deprived of employment and food, was met by local works of a public nature. But the measure which was good and sufficient when applied to limited districts, where such works could easily be found, necessarily fell far short of its object when applied to the whole country, because works such as roads, which were applicable in one district in which roads were wanted, were not of necessity applicable to another – still less to every other district, in the greater part of which roads were already superabundant. Yet to roads, and works of a similar and local character, the public works were confined ... But while it is admitted that merely local works, of the single class to which the relief operations were confined, were unable to meet a distress so general and so long continued, and by which artizans as well as labourers were affected, by which the relations of every class of the community were disturbed, and which involved, and were complicated by, social questions of every description, we have never ceased to express our conviction that this objection of inutility has been greatly overstated, and that the greater part of the works in the remote districts are only such as it would have been desirable at any time to have undertaken, while even in the central and better conditioned counties, the objections which have been made will cease when they are completed.

Nor is it necessary we should repeat that it is not on the ground of positive utility that these works are to be judged. They should be considered solely as an effort to obtain a certain amount of labour in return for subsistence, through the medium of money wages, which effort was not abandoned till the numbers had become so great as to defy control, and to render it indispensable that the subsistence should be given by direct distribution of food, without other condition than that already required – the condition of real destitution. It is not intended to deny the abuses which crept into every part of the system, but we think they may have been greatly exaggerated, and the exception taken for the rule.

When the host had risen to 734,000, it contained large numbers unable to work, and the expenditure for their distress was most judiciously made in food relief. But it should in justice be remembered that the expenditure was still the same. In October, 1846, 100,000 men were employed; nearly the same number remained in the month of June, 1847, and were not wholly discontinued for some months afterwards. The relief by labour, therefore, extended over nine months, the direct relief continued but for three, though the systems were in concurrent operation for a considerable time. The average number relieved daily by labour, from October to June, was 356,314, and the expenditure chargeable to the counties was £4,462,154. 6s.11d., of which one half has been subsequently remitted. The total sum gives, on an average, 1s. per diem to each person, which, assuming him to have contributed to the relief of a family of five, places the cost of the labour relief at 2.5d. per head, for which the repayment of only half is claimed ...

On this subject of expense it may also be desirable here to dispel finally the erroneous impressions which have been entertained as to the cost of staff and plant; and as the accounts have now been closed, the figures are conclusive. The expense under the head of staff and plant amounted to the following percentage of the expenditure:

For pay-clerks and others making payment	1.5 per cent
For tools and implements	1.5 per cent
Check-clerks, overseers, foremen, and gangers	5 per cent

The whole of the superior staff, including the extra establishment in Dublin, having been borne by the government.

Nor should the liberal arrangement which was sanctioned by your Lordships in regard to the tools and implements be unknown to the public. In our early reports we dwelt strongly on the difficulty we experienced in providing a sufficient quantity of tools for the daily increasing throng of labourers, and every accessible source, public and private, was put in requisition for the purpose. But we were also desirous of rendering the manufacture itself a source of relief, and with this view we incurred the inconvenience of taking numerous small contracts in the remote towns and villages of Ireland, rather than procure a more prompt and ready supply by employing the large contractors in England and Scotland. This has been, and still is, the cause of great inconvenience and trouble, from their defective construction, and the endless claims to which it has given rise; but it answered the benevolent purpose sought by it. And when by this means a full equipment was provided for 800,000 labourers of all the various implements likely to be required, the works were ordered to close, and this gigantic mass of stores was left on the hands of the government.

(*Sixteenth Annual Report of the Commissioners of Public Works* (Dublin, 1848); John Killen (ed.), *The Famine Decade: Contemporary Accounts*, (Dublin, 1995), pp. 166–8)

During the course of 1847, relief works began to be scaled down, the government believing them ineffective in coping with the famine crisis. They were largely replaced by food depots, which supplied cooked food, mostly soup, thereby departing from the principles of the 1838 Poor Law Act which dictated that Irish Poor Law Unions could not grant any outdoor relief.

Letter sent by Trevelyan to Lieutenant-Colonel Jones, Chairman of the Board of Works

October 5, 1846

... I hope you will take every practicable precaution to ensure the personal safety of the officers employed under your Board, and I need not add that any expense which may be incurred for this purpose, either in the way of reward to persons who assist in protecting them, or in any other way, will be readily sanctioned.

I can assure you that we shall, *without being in the least deterred by considerations of expense*, establish as many meal stations in the west of Ireland as we can hope to keep regularly supplied; but there is another consideration which must put a decided limit to our operations in this respect, which is, that this year there is a general scarcity over the whole of the United Kingdom and the western countries of Europe, while the prospect of our obtaining any adequate supply from America, or other quarters, is very problematical; and under these circumstances to buy up without restraint supplies intended for the English and Scotch markets would merely have the effect of transferring the famine from a country where the people are fed out of the public purse, to one where they are struggling to maintain themselves; and it would not be tolerated that the English and Scotch labourer should not only have to support the Irish labourers (for it is always the mass of the population which pays the bulk of the taxes), but that the price of the necessaries of life should also be raised upon the former to a famine price by an unrestrained eleemosynary consumption of them in Ireland.

It is of so much importance that correct notions be entertained on this subject, that I will add copious extracts from letters I have recently written to Mr Hewetson and Sir R. Routh, and I shall be obliged to you to lay the whole before your colleagues at the Board.

(BBP (6), *Relief of Distress, Board of Works*, pp. 96–7)

The following instructions on outdoor relief were circulated by Edward Senior, the Assistant Poor Law Commissioner.

Newcastle, October 28, 1846

Gentlemen,

The extreme importance of the general policy of granting out-door relief in the form of one or two meals a-day to poor persons at the workhouse (not inmates) induces me to draw your attention to some facts connected with the subject. Without laying much stress upon the minor objections to this course, such as the possibility of riots, the difficulty of cooking the necessary food for large numbers, with the present limited staff of officers, and small kitchens, the risk of intercourse between the inmates and the outdoor poor, and the spread of contagious diseases and the loss of workhouse property, &c., &c.

I will confine myself to three main objections, first, the moral effect on the poor.

2nd The question as to its legality.

3rd The pecuniary difficulty of raising the necessary rates.

To illustrate the first: The Guardians of the Kilkeel Union, a respectable, intelligent body, and a very fair specimen of a country Union, have resolved to allow tickets to be distributed by the different Guardians each for his own division 'at the common cost of the divisions interested', entitling the bearer to three-quarters of a pound of bread and one pint of soup. They have fixed no maximum as to the number to be relieved, agreed on no class to be excluded from its benefit.

The farmer may and will grant tickets to his own cottiers, the labourer employed on Public Works under the Labour-rate Act, will send his children to be fed at public cost, but the aged, infirm, and sick, who have the strongest claim on our sympathy, will be unable to walk a long distance to the workhouse, and therefore be excluded.

Any one who knows the lower classes in Ireland will agree with me, that this is in other words, feeding the whole body of the poor, in return for no work, subject to no test, with a better and more expensive description of food than they have ever been accustomed to at home in return for labour.

2nd As to the legality. The 41st clause of the Relief Act enables the

Guardians to relieve and set to work *therein* destitute poor after the Commissioners shall have declared the workhouses fit for the reception of the destitute, coupled with the words at the end of the clause giving a preference 'of admission' to the resident over the non-resident if there shall not be sufficient 'accommodation' for all who may apply. The form of registry prescribed by the Act for persons 'admitted into' the work-house, leaves, I think, no doubt that relief given to persons not admitted is illegal.

3rd As to the pecuniary difficulty. It requires fully six months to collect a rate: money can only be obtained during the four winter months when the farmers dispose of their produce. It is absolutely impossible to collect money during the summer; by universal consent (contrary to the Commissioners' Regulations), all rates are now annual, they have nearly all been made and part of them in the process of collection, to increase them could not be done, it would only produce confusion. The estimates for the rates have usually been calculated on a larger number of inmates at an increased weekly cost, but still the calculation is a bare one. It must not be forgotten that the calamity which has beggared the cottier, has reduced the means of the small farmer, who must now eat instead of selling his corn crop. Fully one-third of the rate will, on an average, be lost from this cause. To illustrate this by the Kilkeel case, the expenditure of the Union for the last year was in round numbers £1000, and the new rate was £1200, assuming it all to be collected instead of only two-thirds, but the Guardians owed a debt upwards of £100, consequently, the margin is just £100 to meet double number in the house at an increase expense of half for food alone.

Still, by running into debt with the contractors, they might possibly hold on. If they continue their out-door relief, they will be obliged from absolute want of funds to close their house, and turn out their inmates about March or April, just as the real season of famine commences.

From my accurate knowledge of the pecuniary position of the different Unions, I have no hesitation in saying that there are only two or three Unions in my whole district consisting of large towns which could stand so large a drain on their funds. The collection of the poor-rate has, after a painful struggle, at length been established, and the measure is slowly working its way. To attempt at this moment with double expenditure, and crippled means, the far more extensive experiment of out-door relief, must end in the total failure of the law.

I have, &c.,

(Signed)   *Edward Senior*

Ass. Poor Law Commissioner

To the Poor Law Commissioners

(BBP (1), Reports of the Relief Commissioners, pp. 24–5)

Notice addressed to labourers on Lord Caledon's estate, County Tyrone, announcing the opening of three soup kitchens.

NOTICE

I HEREBY give Notice to the Labourers and Poor Householders on LORD CALEDON'S ESTATE, that his LORDSHIP and LADY CALEDON have instructed me to open

THREE SOUP KITCHENS,

In convenient parts of his Lordship's property, to supply Soup and Bread at a very moderate price ; and that such will be ready for delivery *at Twelve o' Clock, on Monday, the 28th inst.*, at the following places, viz.:

The Model Farm;

The Village of Dyan; and at the

House of J. Marshall, at Bantry Wood;

And will be continued every Day, at the same hour, until further Notice (Sundays excepted).

The Labourers employed at Drainage and other Works, can send their Children to the most convenient of the above places, for a supply of Soup, &c., which shall be sent to them hot in Covered Cans. And in order to encourage useful industry amongst the Children, I hereby offer a Premium of 2d. per Bushel, for Bruised or Pounded Whin Tops, properly prepared as food for Horses and Cows, delivered at any of the above mentioned places.

Lord Caledon has desired his caretakers to permit the Children to gather the Whin Tops on any grounds in his Lordship's possession, particularly in the large Stock Farm of Kedew; and I am sure the Tenantry will also encourage so useful an occupation at the present moment, when it is so desirable to use the strictest economy in the feeding of our Cattle.

HENRY L. PRENTICE

AGENT

NB *A Double supply of Food will be Cooked on Saturdays.*

CALEDON, 19th December 1846

(NAI, RLFC, 3/2, Tyrone)

Extract from Lord John Russell's speech to the House of Commons on the need for a change in government policy, January 1847.

The opinion of the government was ... that the system [of relief works] had become so vast, and, at the same time, the destitution and the want of food had so greatly increased, that it was desirable to attempt some other temporary scheme, by which, if possible, some of the evils which they have now to meet might be mitigated, and with so vast an expenditure of money that more effectual relief should be afforded. It has appeared to us that it will be desirable to form in districts, say, electoral districts, relief committees; which relief committees shall be empowered to receive subscriptions, levy rates, and receive donations from the government; that by means of these they should purchase food and establish soup kitchens in the different districts; that they should, so far as they are able, distribute rations with this purchased food to the famishing inhabitants, and that, furnishing that food, they should not require as indispensable the test of work, but that labouring men should be allowed to work on their own plots of ground or for the farmers, and thus tend to produce food for the next harvest and procure, perhaps, some small wages to enable them to support their families.

After we considered this scheme, I communicated it to the Lord Lieutenant of Ireland [Lord Bessborough]. We have consulted the various officers of the Board of Works and at the head of the Commissiariat. They are prepared to consider it favourably; and we shall endeavour, first by a preparatory measure and next by a bill to be proposed to parliament, to carry into effect this arrangement. There is a person in this country conversant with Ireland, having long been engaged in the public works of that country, who earned not only the general esteem of the governments he has served but of the people among whom his operations were carried on. The person to whom I allude is Sir John Burgoyne ... He will be in communication with the Lord Lieutenant, and will have the co-operation of Colonel Jones and the Board of Works, of the commissariat, the head of the Poor Law Commission, the chief of the constabulary, and of other persons who are competent and ready to give him assistance. In proposing this measure, with the view of affording, if possible, more efficient means of relieving the poor people who are now in want of food, and, at the same time, of setting loose great numbers of persons for the ordinary operations of agriculture, we must take care – and the Lord Lieutenant is prepared to take care – that the substitution of this system for public works shall be made as easy in the transition as possible.

I do not despair of Ireland; I say there is no reason ... why Ireland may not at a future day rise to a state of great happiness and prosperity ...

(*Hansard*, House of Commons (25 January 1847))

Letter to the editor of the Mayo Constitution concerning the tragic events suffered by those who were compelled to walk twenty miles or more seeking outdoor relief. One of the most infamous occurrences in County Mayo during the famine, the tragedy was later annually commemorated by a famine walk from Louisburgh to Delphi.

Louisburgh

April 5th, 1849

Sir – On last Friday, 30th ult., Colonel Hogrove, one of the vice guardians of Westport union, and Captain Primrose, the Poor Law inspector, arrived here on that morning for the purpose of holding an inspection on the paupers who were receiving outdoor relief in this part of the union, but, from some cause or other, they did not, but started off immediately for Delphi Lodge. In a short time after, the relieving officer ordered the poor creatures forthwith to follow him to Delphi Lodge, as he would have them inspected early on the following morning, Saturday, 31st; and in obedience of this humane order, hundreds of these unfortunate living skeletons, men, women and children, might have been seen struggling through the mountain passes and roads for the appointed place. The inspection took place in the morning, and I have been told that nothing could equal the horrible appearance of those truly unfortunate creatures, some of them without a morsel to eat, and others exhausted from fatigue, having travelled upwards of 16 miles to attend the inspection.

It is not for me to say why the inspection took place at Delphi, it being the most remote part of the union, and some of the poor, as I have before stated, having to travel upwards of sixteen miles.

I have now the melancholy duty of informing you and the public, that a woman named Dalton, from Wastelands, six miles to the West of this town, her son and daughter, were all found dead on the road side, on the morning after the inspection, midway between this town and Delphi: and about one mile nearer to this town, two men were found dead – in all, five. The bodies of these ill-fated creatures lay exposed on the road side for three or four days and nights, for the dogs and ravens to feed upon, until some charitable person had them buried in a turf hole at the road side.

Now, Sir, I call upon you, as the sincere friend of the poor, and in the name of that just God who is to judge all at the last day, to call upon the Lord Lieutenant of this county to demand a searching inquiry into this melancholy affair, and prevent, if possible, so many of the poor being sacrificed. If inquests are held, I will let you know the result.

I am, Sir, your obedient servant,

A RATEPAYER

(*Mayo Constitution* (10 April 1849))

Famine Relief in County Galway

	Population in 1841	Maximum no. given food in any one day
Galway	32,511	22,009
Annaghdown	4,941	3,765
Aran	3,521	1,538
Athenry	1,770	1,629
Ballinacourty	3,407	1,136
Claregalway	3,873	2,966
Killanin	11,501	8,952
Lackagh	3,753	3,361
Moycullen	7,343	6,610
Oranmore	4,486	2,792
Oughterard	10,601	10,921
Stradbally	1,264	757

(BBP (8) *Reports of the Relief Commissioners*, p. 322)

Dramatic increases in food prices during the winter of 1846–7 and the failure of public works to cope with the famine crisis placed increased pressure on the Poor Law system, leading to overcrowding in workhouses which had never been designed to cope with the effects of a major famine. One of the main results was the spread of fever which, rather than starvation, was the cause of most deaths during the famine, particularly in the western and south-western regions of the country.

It had only been with the establishment of the Poor Law in 1838 that an effort had been made to alleviate the problems of the poor that was both uniform and country-wide, whereby landlords were expected to support the new system financially. The country was divided into 130 unions, each with a workhouse at its centre. Each union was maintained by a 'poor rate' – a tax levied in the main on the owners of property, rather than the occupiers of land. The union was administered by a Board of Guardians, some of whom were elected by the ratepayers and some of whom, termed ex-officios, were appointed from the highest rated Justices of the Peace presiding in the particular county. The Boards of Guardians had at their disposal certain salaried officers and together they were subject to newly created government departments

When the government decided to abandon special relief measures and transfer responsibility for relief to the Poor Law system, legislation relating to Irish poor relief was reformed in the summer of 1847 (described below by Trevelyan), leading to the establishment of a separate Irish Poor Law Commission. The number of existing Poor Law unions increased from 130 to 163 and the 'Gregory Clause' was introduced, which denied public relief to those holding more than a quarter of an acre of land.

A disproportionate number of workhouse inmates were women and children, and many workhouses were compelled to erect temporary accommodation. Poor Law guardians had to follow strict guidelines before admittance could be granted. Numbers in receipt of Poor Law assistance peaked in 1849, exacerbated by evictions and the Gregory Clause, which forced many to either forsake their land or attempt to transfer ownership temporarily. The problems of operating assistance were made more difficult by the fact that the burden of relief, in the form of poor rates, fell most heavily on those districts least able to pay.

The phrase 'Famine Fever' covered a multitude of diseases, of which typhus, relapsing fever and dysentery were the most widespread. The Central Board of Health was appointed by the government early in 1847 to deal with these fever epidemics. The workhouse infrastructure, which had originally been built to accommodate 80,000 people – or 1 per cent of the population – was swamped by famine destitution. According to the census of 1851, on the night of 30 March 1851, 250,611 people – or one in 26 of the population of Ireland – were paupers receiving indoor poor relief, in either workhouses, auxillary workhouses or workhouse hospitals.

Three things had become apparent before the close of the year 1846. The first was that if these gigantic efforts were much longer continued they must exhaust and disorganize society throughout the United Kingdom, and reduce all classes of people in Ireland to a state of helpless dependence. The second was that provision ought to be made for the relief of extreme destitution in some less objectionable mode than that which had been adopted, for want of a better, under the pressure of an alarming emergency. The third was that great efforts and great sacrifices were required to provide another and a better subsistence for the large population which had hitherto depended upon the potato.

Upon these principles the plan of the Government for the season of 1847–8, and for all after-time, was based. Much the larger portion of the machinery of a good Poor Law had been set up in Ireland by the Irish Poor Relief Act which was passed in the year 1838. The island has been divided into unions, which were generally so arranged as to secure easy communication with the central station; and these had been subdivided into electoral districts, each of which appointed its own guardian, and was chargeable only with its own poor, like our parishes. A commodious workhouse had also been built in each union by advances from the Exchequer, and rates had been established for its support. No relief could, however, be given outside the workhouses, and when these buildings once became filled with widows and children, aged and sick, and others who might with equal safety and more humanity have been supported at their own homes, they ceased to be either a medium of relief or a test of destitution to the other destitute poor of the union.

To remedy this and other defects of the existing system, three acts of parliament were passed in the session of 1847, the principal provisions of which were as follows: destitute persons who are either permanently or temporarily disabled from labour, and destitute widows having two or more legitimate children dependent upon them, may be relieved either in or out of the workhouse, at the discretion of the guardians. If, owing to want of a room, or to the prevalence of fever or any infectious disorder, adequate relief cannot be afforded in a workhouse to persons not belonging to either of the above-mentioned classes, the Poor Law Commissioners may authorize the guardians to give them outdoor relief in food only; the Commissioners' order for which purpose can only be made for a period of two months, but, if necessary, it can be renewed from time to time. Relieving officers and medical officers for affording medical relief out of the workhouse are to be appointed; and in cases of sudden and urgent necessity, the relieving officers are to give 'immediate and temporary relief in food, lodging, medicine, or medical attendance' until the next meeting of the guardians. After the 1st November, 1847, no person is to be relieved either in or out of a workhouse, who is in the occupation of more than a quarter of an acre of land.

(Trevelyan, *The Irish Crisis*, pp. 151–4)

Report by Constable John Norris, Aughrim, County Wicklow, 16 June 1847, describing the circumstances in which he found a fever-stricken woman and child on the roadway near Aughrim.

Co. of Wicklow

Aughrim, June 16 1847

I have to state that on the 11th inst. a travelling pauper named Honor Kerwin and her child dropped on the highway near Aughrim, both being ill with fever and lay on the side of the road till the following day when I reported the case to Jeremiah Tool the warden, who had them conveyed to Rathdrum Fever Hospital immediately. But being refused admittance there they were sent back to this place and left on the cross roads at Aughrim the most past of the night and then put into a shed. On the following day (Monday) I informed Doctor Atkins of the case who gave a certificate stating the poor woman had fever and was a fit object for the Fever Hospital.

The Revd Mr Malony and two cess payers [rate payers] recommended them to the Fever Hospital also. These recommendations together with the warden's note was forwarded the same day, with the poor woman, to Arklow Fever Hospital and (she) was also refused admittance there stating they should 'have been sent to Rathdrum' and had them conveyed back to Aughrim and left on the cross roads for a night to the great danger of the people of this neighbourhood.

On Tuesday myself and two of this party with some others of the neighbours procured timber and erected a shed and put the two sick persons in to it and went through the neighbours and got a few pence to get them nourishment for them and also procured a nurse tender to take care of them. It is a very hard case that there is no place to remove poor persons of this description when they fall on the public roads and although I am well aware it is no part of my duty to interfere in such cases. Still every person calls me to keep the public passways clear of such nuisances. There is 8 or 9 families at present ill with fever in this neighbourhood, some of them in sheds and no place to receive them. I hope you will see if there is any remedy to this state of things.

John Norris
Constable

(NAI, RLFC, Miscellaneous papers)

Correspondence between Sir George Grey, Home Secretary 1846–52, and Edward Twisleton, who was Chief Poor Law Commissioner 1847–9.

Whitehall December 21, 1846

... I need scarcely say, that I fully appreciate the difficulties with which you have to contend, but I much regret to observe that you consider, that although special powers applicable to cases of emergency, are given by the Poor Relief Act for making additional provision to a certain extent for the relief of the destitute, such powers cannot now be exercised, owing to the difficulty of collecting a rate. And it appears that in the Union of Ballina, in consequence of these powers not having been exercised, deaths have been reported in cases where the deceased persons had sought admission to the workhouse and been refused from want of room. I am unable to acquiesce in the property of abstaining under such circumstances from an attempt to put into force those powers which the legislature has provided for cases of extraordinary pressure, and I feel that a very heavy responsibility rests on those who, from declining to exercise their powers, refuse to persons without any other means of support, that relief which ought to be afforded them. If on the allegation, that great difficulty exists in collecting the rate at present outstanding and that the collection of any new rate, except from the better class of ratepayer, is next to impossible, 'external aid', by which I presume is meant aid from the public treasury, is to be afforded to the Board of Guardians, I fear the inevitable result would be, that the alleged difficulty or impossibility would become general if not universal and the Boards of Guardians would at once throw upon the government the responsibility which by law attaches to themselves. I entertain, therefore, the strongest objection to any grant from the public treasury in aid of or as a substitute for the rate for the relief of the poor. Whatever aid the government may give, should, in my opinion, be distinct from and independent of the funds administered under the Poor Law and should be applied to the relief of those cases which cannot be provided for under the Poor Relief Act when brought into the fullest operation. Many persons liable to be rated are, if my information is correct, at the present time placing their money in the savings banks, and by their refusal to employ any labourers in the cultivation of their land, are increasing the existing distress. To acquiesce in their exemption from the burden legally and morally attaching to them, would I think, be most objectionable in principle and most injurious in its effect ...

To which Mr Twisleton replied:

In reference to your letter of the 21st instant, I am desirous of offering a few remarks on deposits in savings banks, as indicators of the prosperity or distress of a district. Circumstances induced me to pay considerable attention to the subject in 1842 and 1843, and I am convinced that there are few social questions on which such erroneous ideas are prevalent. Within the last six weeks there have been leading articles in *The Times* and *Morning Chronicle* on the state of the Irish savings banks, which, probably, produced a considerable impression on the public mind. One of these articles in particular, which displayed remarkable ability, and was written, I have no doubt, in good faith, according to the knowledge of the writer, seemed to treat the increase in the deposits as a proof of successful swindling on the part of the Irish people during the past year.

I well know, however, through fallacy of the assumption on which the article was based, and could not but deplore the mischief which such views were likely to occasion. Now, it would be a serious misfortune if Her Majesty's Government, amidst the multiplicity of subjects which are likely to occupy their attention, were led to suppose that these views rested on a foundation of truth. I, therefore, am anxious to say a few words on the subject. So far from it being necessarily true that an increase in the deposits of savings banks negatives accounts of distress in a district, the direct reverse may be the case and the increase of deposits may be a symptom that severe distress exists and is apprehended. This arises from the following circumstances. When times begin to be bad, as it is called, the deposits may increase in the following ways:

1. Individuals in employment, who had been thoughtless previously, and did not save money at all, may become depositors for the first time.

2. Individuals in employment, who previously were depositors, may increase their deposits.

3. Thrifty individuals, who otherwise may have invested their little savings in small speculations, feel an uncertainty as to the probable return, and have recourse to savings banks, because the interest given by them for deposits is certain.

4. Individuals of a higher class than those who previously made use of savings banks (say, for example, employers of labour) cease to employ labourers and become depositors.

It is true that some individuals in distress may withdraw their deposits; but this may be far more than compensated by the increase, owing to the above causes: Just as a calamitous fire, even when the property burnt has been insured, may be a source of gain to the insurance office of a district.

It is by no means intended, by the above remarks, to assert that increase in the deposits in savings banks may not arise from the prosperity of a district, or that long continued distress may not occasion an absolute decrease. The object is merely to show that such increase may likewise arise from distress, so that no inference can be safely drawn, either one way or the other, from the mere fact of the increase.

In order to be justified in drawing any inference, it is requisite to make a special study of all the circumstances and to ascertain not only the classes of persons who deposited the money but likewise their motives. I will add, that if, since the harvest of 1845 (up to which period the physical property of Ireland seemed to be gradually, although slowly advancing), there has been distress in this country, an increase in the deposits of savings banks is precisely what might have been anticipated ...

(BPP (12 and 17), *State of the Unions and Workhouses*)

Notice issued by the Roscommon Poor Law Guardians, suspending admission to the workhouse.

NOTICE

ROSCOMMON UNION

Notice is hereby given, that the State of the Poor House, both from Excessive Numbers and Sickness, makes it absolutely necessary for the Guardians to proclaim the utter impossibility to admit any more persons until further notice.

The Guardians have on two occasions given a small portion of Bread to disappointed applicants; but after this Notice, it can never be done again, such expenditure being illegal, and possibly may not be allowed by the Auditor of the Poor Law Commissioners.

By Order of the Guardians,

John Corr, Clerk of the Union

January 9th, 1847

(NAI, RLFC, II/2b 9837)

The following report from a local doctor, describing how he found a family of six in a small hut, stricken by fever, was published in the Illustrated London News *in 1847.*

On my return home, I remembered that I had yet a visit to pay; having in the morning received a ticket to see six members of one family, named Barrett, who had been turned out of the cabin in which they lodged, in the neighbourhood of Old Chapelyard; and who had struggled to this burying ground, and literally entombed themselves in a small watch-house that was built for the shelter of those who were engaged in guarding against exhumation by the doctors when more respect was paid to the dead than is at present the case. This shed is exactly seven feet long, by about six in breadth. By the side of the western wall is a long, newly made grave; by either gable are two of shorter dimensions, which have been recently tenanted; and near the hole that serves as a doorway is the last resting place of two or three children; in fact, this hut is surrounded by a rampart of human bones, which have accumulated to such a height that the threshold, which was originally on a level with the ground, is now two feet beneath it. In this horrible den, in the midst of a mass of human putrefaction, six individuals, males and females, labouring under most malignant fever, were huddled together, as closely as were the dead in the graves around.

(*Illustrated London News*, 13 February 1847)

An account of conditions in the Ballinrobe workhouse in County Mayo

In Ballinrobe the workhouse is in the most awfully deplorable state, pestilence having attacked paupers, officers, and all. In fact, this building is one horrible charnel house, the unfortunate paupers being nearly all the victims of a fearful fever, the dying and the dead, we might say, huddled together. The master has become the victim of this dread disease; the clerk, a young man whose energies were devoted to the well-being of the union, has been added to the victims; the matron, too, is dead; and the respected and esteemed physician has fallen before the ravages of pestilence, in his constant attendance on the diseased inmates.

This is the position of the Ballinrobe house, every officer swept away, while the number of deaths among the inmates is unknown; and we forgot to add that the Roman Catholic chaplain is also dangerously ill of the same epidemic. Now the Ballinrobe board have complied with the Commissioners' orders, in admitting a houseful of paupers and in striking a new rate, which cannot be collected; while the unfortunate inmates, if they escape the awful epidemic, will survive only to be the subjects of a lingering death by starvation!

We have heard also of the inmates of the Westport workhouse and several of the officers being attacked by fever, but fortunately without any fatal results. Ballina and Swinford, too, have not escaped the dreadful contagion, and Sligo has been fearfully scourged. The master – for many years a colour sergeant of the 88th Regiment, who fought through many a bloody field unscathed – has fallen before dire disease, and the paupers are dying in dozens.

(*Mayo Constitution* (23 March 1847))

Circular issued by the Central Board of Health, Dublin, on 17 May 1847 to local relief committees, describing precautions to be taken in order to prevent the spread of fever.

Applications having been made to the Central Board of Health, to put in force those provisions of the Fever Act, 10 Victoria, chap. 2, which relate to measures for the prevention of Fever, such as the cleansing and purifying of the habitations of the poor and the removal of nuisances etc., and for the proper and decent interment of the dead, the Board of Health deem it necessary to draw the attention of the various Relief Committees to sections IX and XVI of the said Act, from which it will be seen that the Board of Health are not authorized to issue any order or enforce any measures in relation to the cleansing, Ventilating and Purifying of the Habitations of the poor, the removal of Nuisances, or the interment of the dead. These duties are devolved by the Act wholly on the respective Relief Committees throughout the Country, who are armed with ample powers for the purpose, without needing any authority from the Board of Health [which] can do no more at present than offer some general suggestions.

1st. In reference to the provisions of Clause IX. For Cleansing and purifying the Habitations of the poor, and for the removal of nuisances. The present time appears to be a favourable opportunity for enabling relief committees to effect these objects with little expense, as the services of a sufficient number of able-bodied destitute persons now receiving gratuitous outdoor relief, can probably be obtained for a trifling addition of Rations or Money, who can be employed under proper superintendence, in whitewashing the rooms and passages of the habitations of the poor, and in removing nuisances, such as collections of manure, contents of ash-pits etc. In whitewashing, the regulation should be strictly enforced of having the lime always slacked immediately previously to using it, and of laying on the whitewash while still hot ...

2nd. In reference to inducing cleanliness of clothing and person among the poor, – measures so essential to health and the prevention of infection. A rule has been adopted in some instances, of insisting upon all applicants for gratuitous relief coming to the provision depots with at least face, hands, and hair clean. This regulation has been attended with good results. The Board of Health, however, thinks that the principle might be carried further, with great advantage, and that habits of cleanliness might be rapidly induced, if in every district in convenient localities Washing houses on a simple and economical plan were established, to be kept open for a certain number of hours per day ...

3rd. The separation of the sick from the healthy. The early removal of the sick to hospital is a measure of the greatest importance in checking the spread of disease. To effect this with expedition and certainty, arrangements must be made –

1st. For procuring the earliest intimation of the appearance of illness.

2nd. For the removal of persons affected.

To attain the first object, printed papers should be posted up requesting the poor to give immediate notice of the first appearance of illness in their families, at the gate of the hospital, where the porter, or a person appointed for the purpose, should keep a book in which he may enter the name and residences of the applications for admission ... There should be in cities or towns, as in former epidemics, one or more medical inspectors, according to the extent, for each hospital district, whose duty it should be to visit, as soon as possible, the cases reported each morning, and such other cases as they may hear of, and to return to the office by a certain hour a list of those persons who are fit subjects for removal to hospital. On the lists being returned, a light covered vehicle should be in readiness to convey the sick to hospital in the course of the same day. The books kept as above, will, besides, be most useful in affording information as to the actual state of disease, its diminution or increase in each district, and the corresponding amount of information required.

4th. Interment of the dead – on the provisions of Clause XVI. The Board of Health deems it necessary to offer only the following suggestions: That graves should invariably be sunk to a depth of five feet; that the surface of each grave should be beaten hard; that where burials have already taken place, leaving the coffins nearer to the surface than five feet, clay should be carted in to cover the graves to a sufficient depth, and that, wherever obtainable, yellow clay should be preferred for this purpose; and, finally, that when new grave-yards are opened, localities should be selected at least a quarter of a mile from any town, village, or hospital, in a sufficiently exposed situation to prevent the accumulation of malaria ...

(NAI, M 3487)

Freeman's Journal leading article on the prevalence of 'Famine Fever' in Dublin.

We have the best authority in stating that in one parish in this city there are no less than 1,000 patients ill of fever. The new cases in the same locality average thirty daily. This melancholy state of things is to be attributed principally to two causes: want of hospital accommodation and the use of unwholesome food ... While fever patients pine, writhe and perish, among the close pestilential atmosphere of crowded lanes and alleys, spreading the disease, and dragging all who come in contact with them down to share their untimely graves. Cork Street Hospital is closed, though there is said to be still within its walls unoccupied accommodation. But the most melancholy feature of this sad state of things yields in power of appalling when compared with the heartless cruelty of meting out to the poor food from the bare sight of which one shrinks in horror.

Two specimens of this life-destroying charity-bread has been sent to our office. The test sample came to us from where it was being distributed, the relief depot, Bridge Street; and we purpose to send it for inspection to the office of the Relief Commissioners. It is a kind of bread, black, mouldy, and of most noisome smell. It was made by the cook appointed under the Relief Commissioners. Two hundred loaves of this poisonous stuff were, we are informed, distributed for rations on the occasion the specimen sent to us was doled out! Need we be surprised to learn that fever is spreading when such predisposing causes, in the use of unwholesome food, exist? Need we wonder that fever, coming forth from the dens of squalid misery where it usually lurks, assails, 'as a giant refreshed from wine', the higher classes; and, like the destroying angel, slays a victim in almost every house, when those higher classes tamely look on the deeds that are being done in the case of the poor? It should seem to be a wise ordination of providence that, when the higher classes permit famine to slay the poor, pestilence arises from that slaughter and slays the higher classes in turn ...

(*Freeman's Journal* (27 July 1847))

One of the many coroners' verdicts delivered during the famine, in November 1847.

George Nixon, of Ballyjames Duff, surgeon, deposeth – I saw Catherine McEvoy *alias* Mullin about a month since last alive, when I examined the body of her son, on whom an inquest was holden, and whose death had been accelerated from destitution and exposure to the severity of the weather. I have examined the body of Catherine Mullin, find no marks of violence; the outer surface of the body bears evident marks of emaciation, and I am of opinion that her death was accelerated from want of sufficient nutriment, and exposure to the inclemency of the severe weather, having had no covering to the hut, save a few branches. I am of opinion that she had no inordinate appetite (which is a disease in itself), but that her craving for food, as stated by the evidence, was the result of the want of a sufficient supply.

I am also of opinion, if immediate relief is not afforded her surviving child, he must immediately share the same fate of his mother and brother.
George Nixon
Surgeon

Verdict. – We find that Catherine Mullin (*alias* McEvoy), aged 43 years, was found dead in a hut the 23rd of November, 1847. We are of opinion that she died from want of sufficient nutriment and exposure to cold, and that her son, aged six years, will share the same fate except some relief be given him immediately.
John Macfadin
Coroner

(BPP (2) 4th and 5th Series, *State of the Unions and Workhouses*, 1847–9)

Count Paul Edmund de Strzelecki's correspondence with the Poor Law Commissioners, 31 July 1848. Count Strzelecki was a member of the British Association which had been established in January 1847 in the City of London to help alleviate the famine crisis, with the backing of Lord Russell and, in particular, Trevelyan, who encouraged its evangelical philanthropic ethos.

... I beg to enclose, for the information of the Poor Law Commissioners, a statement showing the periods in which, according to the opinion of the Poor Law Inspectors, the relief to children should stop in their respective Unions.

Enclosure.

Statement showing the date at which the Poor Law Inspectors recommend that the Relief to Children should be closed :

Unions in Which the Relief is to be Closed on the 20th August

No.	Name of Unions	Number of Children
1	Ballina	14,291
2	Belmullet	3,683
3	Ballinrobe	7,023
4	Ballyshannon	8,185
5	Bantry	9,411
6	Cahirciveen	2,614
7	Castlebar	4,858
8	Clifden	4,226
9	Donegal	5,955
10	Galway	4,618
11	Glenties	6,211
12	Kenmare	4,213
13	Skibbereen	19,141
14	Swineford	19,064
15	Tuam	4,640
16	Westport	8,380
	Total	**126,513**

(BBP, *Proceedings for the Relief of the Distress*, 7th series (1848), Miscellaneous)

An editorial from the Illustrated London News *expressing sympathy with landowners struggling under the weight of the Poor Law.*

... If they were a wealthy body of men, they might lighten [the poor rate] effectually, by draining and otherwise improving their estates, and converting their paupers into labourers. But, as they are an impoverished body of men, they will endeavour to improve their estates by the best means which they can employ. It does not require any very large or difficult expenditure of capital to clear them of the cottier population, or convert small holdings into large farms, to be cultivated in the English and Scottish style of agriculture. It is the easiest mode of improvement, and, therefore, poor landlords are compelled to resort to it ... now that a Poor Law has been introduced, we have no right, how great soever the apparent or real hardship may be, to find fault with the landlord, or cry out against his cruelty for dispossessing and ejecting the miserable swarms who encumber his land, and drag him into pauperism as bad as their own.

(*Illustrated London News* (16 December 1848))

The tables of deaths revealed in the census of 1851 brought home the scale of fever-related mortality.

... Some approximation to the amount of the immense mortality that prevailed may be gleaned from the published tables, which show that within the calamitous period between the end of 1845 and the conclusion of the first quarter of 1851, as many as 61,260 persons died in the hospitals and sanitary institutions, exclusive of those who died in the Workhouses and auxillary Workhouses. Taking the recorded deaths from fever alone, between the beginning of 1846 and the end of 1849, and assuming the mortality at one in ten, which is the very lowest calculation, and far below what we believe really did occur, above a million and a half, or 1,595,040 persons, being one in 4.11 of the population in 1851, must have suffered from fever during that period. But no pen has recorded the numbers of the forlorn and starving who perished by the wayside or in the ditches, or of the mournful groups, sometimes of whole families, who lay down and died, one after another, upon the floor of their miserable cabins, and so remained uncoffined and unburied, till chance unveiled the appalling scene. No such amount of suffering and misery has been chronicled in Irish history since the days of Edward Bruce, and yet, through all, the forbearance of the Irish peasantry, and the calm submission with which they bore the deadliest ills that can fall on man, can scarcely be paralleled in the annals of any people ...

(*Census of Ireland for the Year 1851*; 'Report on *Tables of Deaths*'; O'Rourke, *History*, p. 482)

Amount of Poor Rate Collected during Each Month in the Three Years Ending September 1848

	1846	1847	1848
	£	£	£
October	27,605	26,805	121,255
November	30,792	36,639	151,684
December	33,262	46,440	168,850
January	36,229	52,439	194,054
February	41,885	47,264	187,064
March	38,909	52,561	138,449
April	38,436	63,110	111,981
May	31,230	64,865	114,518
June	30,630	59,436	121,571
July	24,185	62,197	95,452
August	17,173	53,389	102,107
September	21,510	73,358	120,715
Total	**371,846**	**638,503**	**1,627,700**

(BBP (1), *State of the Unions and Workhouses*, p. 217)

The following are extracts from reports by Joseph Burke, Poor Law Commissioner, who travelled extensively to assess the state of workhouses.

No. 1079: Prevailing Distress, Cork Union, 12 November 1846

Gentlemen,

I trust it may not be deemed beyond my duty in offering as I have hitherto done suggestions as to relieving the distress which unhappily prevails. The opportunities which I have of witnessing, through a very extensive district, the present condition of the people and judging of their future prospects, afforded me information on the subject which may not be open to or taken advantage of by others – although bad as is the state of the people I dread that it will be worse next year – the small farmers and the cottiers are obliged to sacrifice their future means of support to providing the means of their present existence, neglecting the culture of their small farms and gardens and getting or looking after employment on the public works – the larger farmers are sowing wheat and if the small farmers and cottiers were to sow rye, bere and potatoes (those digging out being only fit for trying the experiment) things might not be so bad next year. But unfortunately the small farms and gardens all lie uncultivated and unsown, and to think that a people whose whole thoughts are fixed on, as I have said, proving means for their present existence will be able to do this is quite out of the question. I would suggest that rye and bere seed be procured and furnished to relief committees or to the offices of the board of public works – that the people now on the public work be employed for the ensuing month in sowing in every available spot which the small farmer or cottier may wish to have sown with rye and bere and potatoes, if the seed of the latter be supplied by such small farmer or cottier during the ensuing month – if the weather which I trust it may should be fine – great good will be effected in this way – the present and future wants of the people, the former by work and the latter by food will be provided for. Rye will grow in boglands, bere in any middling upland soil; but luxuriously in potato soil – both crops will come in early in June at the most trying season. There are many details which I have not leisure now to enter into with respect to this place but which can be easily arranged. The Relief Committee can judge of the parties to whom this free labour and seed may be supplied. The work could be superintended by the officers of the Board of Public Works who could have the men in groups going from holding to holding. This would be preferable for the sake of the superintendence to having a few working together. Fifty or a hundred acres a day may be sown in a district and the produce of this early next summer would be a most welcome provision to the people ...

No. 1120: Skibbereen Union, Mortality in Workhouse, Bandon, 13 January 1847

Gentlemen,

I forward herewith a letter dated 19th instant from Dr Donavan, the medical attendant of the workhouse of the Skibbereen Union in which he states that there is so much disease in the workhouse and so great a likelihood that it will continue he will require some medical assistance in the discharge of his duties and that the services of a professional gentleman may be had at Skibbereen. I beg to recommend that a letter be addressed to the Board of Guardians bringing under their consideration Dr Donavan's application.

No. 1127: Prevailing Distress, Cork Union, 18 January 1847

Gentlemen,

I this day attended the meeting of the Guardians of the Cork Union. The number of inmates in the workhouse and in the two additional wards has now reached 5310 – 868 of whom were admitted within the last fortnight – the medical officers, having given in their report, a copy of which I forward, the propriety of allowing further admissions was discussed, where it was agreed not to exceed the present number in the house and that admissions could only be allowed as discharges occurred. A proposition to revert again to the practice of giving a meal a day to persons not inmates of the workhouse who might apply for it was made but met with no support ... It appears from the great demand at present for stores that no further accommodation can be procured. In addition to the two buildings already taken, the guardians agreed to adopt a suggestion in the medical officers' report of erecting temporary wooden sheds – the plans and estimate for which I also forward, and should they meet your approval beg that a form of consent for this expenditure may be sent to the clerk for the signatures of a majority of the guardians. A resolution was also adopted by the guardians that the present poor law was quite inadequate to meet the unprecedented destitution which now prevails. It must certainly be admitted that the poor law was introduced to meet the destitution of an ordinary year – but not to provide against a famine. If the Guardians of the Cork Union could procure further accommodation I am certain that the numbers that would avail themselves of workhouse relief would be double or treble what it is now – and then would come the question of how funds were to be procured, as adequate means to meet such an extensive system of relief could not be obtained by making heavy rates on an impoverished people ...

I am Gentlemen,

Your obedient servant,

Joseph Burke

Assistant Commissioner

No. 1149: Macroon Union, State of Workhouse, Macroon, 3 February 1847

Gentlemen, '

I this day inspected the workhouse of the Macroon Union, to which I was accompanied by the medical officer, master and the acting master – the Guardians having admitted inmates far beyond the number recommended by the medical officer – illness in consequence prevails through the house – the master and schoolmistress are laid up in fever and the workhouse books have not been regularly kept or made up for the last fortnight. I can therefore only give the number in the house for the mere supposition of the young man who is acting master who states it at 1400. I have however this day given instructions to him as to how he could make up the books – the schoolmaster died recently of old age and disability. I never beheld a more wretched looking set of beings than those who have been recently admitted and who, to add to the irregularity of this house, are all in their own clothes and no chance from the state of the funds of the Union, of their being supplied with house clothing. The Guardians have taken a store near the workhouse as an additional ward which I visited today in company with the medical officer who states that it will with safety lodge about 130 inmates. I forward a report on the sanitary state of the workhouse from the medical officer who is most zealous and attentive in the discharge of the very onerous duties which now devolve upon him. I propose returning here on Friday and attending the Board on the following day after which I shall again have the honour of reporting to you on the state of the workhouse.

I am, gentlemen, etc.

No. 1532: Enniscorthy and Wexford Union, 21 October 1848

Gentlemen,

I beg to refer you to the resolution in Minutes of Proceedings of the Guardians of the Enniscorthy Union of the 17th instant and to accompanying papers in relation to it. By this you will see that the Guardians of the Wexford Union refused relief to two destitute paupers named Peter Roche and Daniel Cleary, both of whom had been previously residing in the Wexford Union, on the grounds that they did not belong to the Union. I also forward a resolution this day adopted by the Guardians of the Enniscorthy Union relative to the matter, and although I impressed on the Guardians of the latter union that they were bound even under the circumstance to afford relief to those persons, all I could get the Guardians to consent to was to afford provisional relief to them for a day or two, and that the parties could then proceed to Wexford to make further applications to the Guardians of that Union. It is most unreasonable that these poor people should be sent in this way from Union to Union without getting relief and as the Guardians of the Wexford Union in the first instance acted wrong in refusing it, I beg to suggest that a letter be addressed to them, referring to your circular of the 29th December 1847 on this subject and pointing out to the Guardians the erroneous view they seem to have taken of the matter ...

(NAI, Poor Law Commissioners, 2/440/45)

Asenath Nicholson's record of the famine, published in London in 1850, was one of a number of eyewitness accounts during the period. A Presbyterian evangelist, she was born in Vermont in the late eighteenth century, where she worked as a teacher before moving to New York. She arrived in Ireland in June 1844.

A cabin was seen closed one day a little out of the town, when a man had the curiosity to open it, and in a dark corner he found a family of the father, mother and two children, lying in close compact. The father was considerably decomposed; the mother, it appeared, had died last, and probably fastened the door, which was always the custom when all hope was extinguished, to get into the darkest corner and die, where passers-by could not see them. Such family scenes were quite common, and the cabin was generally pulled down upon them for a grave. The man called, begging me to look in. I did not, and could not endure, as the famine progressed, such sights, as well as at the first, they were too real, and these realities became a dread. In all my former walks over the island, by day or night, no shrinking or fear of danger ever retarded in the least my progress; but no, the horror of meeting living walking ghosts, or stumbling upon the dead in my path at night, inclined me to keep within when necessity did not call ...

(Asenath Nicholson, *Lights and Shades of Ireland* (London, 1850), p. 330.)

Reported Starvation Deaths in Selected Counties, 1844–50

County	1844	1845	1846	1847	1848	1849	1850
Kildare	0	2	3	2	4	8	14
Meath	1	4	11	23	31	27	21
Clare	13	20	44	133	238	286	241
Kerry	15	20	123	586	270	296	184
Donegal	5	6	44	99	49	32	17
Fermanagh	3	7	34	103	25	17	7
Mayo	51	79	293	927	885	784	373
Roscommon	8	20	123	480	306	188	65

Deaths Recorded from Main Killer Diseases in Workhouses, 1845–50

Year	Fever	Dysentery	Diarrhoea	Starvation	Total Deaths	Ratio of Deaths to Number Relieved
1845	421	391	415	4	5,979	1 in 19.10
1846	1,334	1,354	1,358	8	14,662	1 in 17.11
1847	10,397	13,531	4,760	83	66,890	1 in 6.62
1848	6,645	9,500	3,081	56	45,482	1 in 13.42
1849	7,026	12,602	5,316	73	64,440	1 in 14.47
1850	6,478	9,238	3,555	63	46,721	1 in 17.24

(Census of Ireland for the Year 1851; Liam Kennedy, Paul Ell, E. M. Crawford and L. A. Crawford (eds.), Mapping the Great Irish Famine (Dublin, 1999), p.128)

Total Numbers Relieved in the Workhouses, 1844–53

Year	Number of Workhouses	Number of people Relieved
1844	113	105,358
1845	123	114,205
1846	130	243,933
1847	131	417,139
1848	131	610,463
1849	131	932,284
1850	163	805,702
1851	163	707,443
1852	163	504,864
1853	163	396,438

(George Nicholls, A History of the Irish Poor Law (London, 1856), pp. 323 and 395; Kennedy et al, Mapping the Great Irish Famine, p. 125)

Catholic priests had a particular role to play in articulating the grievances of famine victims and indeed in documenting the sights they experienced, not just as pastors of their communities but also as some of the more literate members of Irish society. Most were the sons of relatively prosperous farmers and not as dependent on the potato as labourers and cottiers, though income in most parishes would have plummeted and bishops were under pressure to reduce the number of priests serving in the dioceses.

The account of his daily life by Hugh Quigley, curate in Killaloe.

We rise at four o'clock ... when not obliged to attend a night call ... and ... proceed on horseback a distance of from four to seven miles to hold stations of confession for the convenience of the poor country people, who ... flock in thousands ... to prepare themselves for the death they look to as inevitable. At these stations we have to remain up to five o'clock p.m. administering both consolation and instruction to the famishing households ... the confessions are often interrupted by calls to the dying, and generally, on our way home we have to ... administer the last rites ... to one or more fever patients. Arrived at home, we have scarcely seated ourselves to a little dinner, when we are interrupted by groans and sobs of several persons at the door, crying out, 'I am starving', 'If you do not help me I must die' and 'I wish I was dead', etc ... In truth the priest must either harden his heart against the cry of misery, or deprive himself of his usual nourishment to keep victims from falling at his door. After dinner – or, perhaps before it is half over – the priest is again surrounded by several persons, calling on him to come in his haste – that their parents, or brothers, or wives, or children, are 'just departing'. The priest is again obliged to mount his jaded pony, and endeavour to keep pace with the peasant who trots before him as a guide, through glen and ravine, and over precipice, to his infected hut ... the curate has most commonly to say two masses ... at different chapels; and ... to preach patience and resignation to the people, to endeavour to prevent them rising *en masse* and plundering and murdering their landlords. This gives but a faint idea of the life of a priest here, leaving scarcely any time for prayer or meditation ...

(Donal Kerr, The Catholic Church and the Famine (Dublin, 1996), pp. 19–20)

The following was written on 27 December 1846 by W. Millikin, a relief commissioner, from the relief district of Moycullen in Galway, denying the claim made by a local priest that there was widespread starvation in his parish.

With reference to your letter no.13 directing me to enquire into the real destitution now prevailing in the Barony of Moycullen in consequence of a strong application having been made to his excellency the Lord Lieutenant by Rev. Myr Phew, Roman Catholic curate from Lettermullen. I have the honour to report that on my return from Connemara I visited that locality, found Mr Phew at the village of Moycullen having been removed from his other charge some months since ... as the Barony of Moycullen is considered one of the richest in this part of Galway, on account of the rich crops of wheat that are raised, and as I could not perceive any visible distress or destitution and the locality being so near this, had it existed to the extent described by him, it would have been laid before the Committee at Oughterard or Galway. I therefore continued my inquiries to other channels, the constabulary, proprietors, etc., and am happy to state after taking every pains to ascertain the truth – that less destitution exists in that parish than any other in this district and less probability of the evil returning next season for they have more wheat sown than anywhere else. The Reverend Gentleman is notorious for making himself conspicuous and is exceedingly fond of writing to the higher authorities. He was removed from Lettermullen for sending in an exaggerated account of the starving state of the population at that place. This I had from one of the proprietors and confirmed by an English clergyman and I have witnessed so much of the kind at the relief committees, [with] the Catholic Clergy trying to monopolise the whole of the labour on the public works for their own flocks and recommending persons not in a state of absolute destitution. The only thing that can be stated in mitigation [is] that unless the people get money, the priests will be equally paupers as their stipends depend almost entirely from that source ...

(NAI, RLFC 7/11/04)

Bernard Duncan, parish priest in Swinford, County Mayo, wrote the following to the Chief Secretary.

Swinford is the centre of an extensive and densely populated district as poor as any in Ireland. There is not a single resident landlord in the barony (Gallen) of which it is the chief town, who can give the least relief, or agent who takes any interest in procuring it. There was a depot established in it for the sale of Indian corn and oatmeal in small quantities, from which, whilst the supply was kept up, much advantage was derived, as the people had the opportunity of getting even the smallest quantity at a moderate price and the markets were kept down. But alas! They have been deprived of even this advantage. There has been no meal in the depot for the last ten days nor are there any hopes held out of its being continued at all. The consequence is that oatmeal which, while the depot was in operation, sold for 16s. or 17s. a cwt, has risen in the local markets to £1 2s. I am told that the reason for giving up the depot is that the people are supposed to have the oat crop now available. It is true the greater part of the holders of land have; but then there are thousands of poor families who have no land or who, having a small portion of boggy land, have no oats and these, having no employment for the last six months and no earthly means of procuring any food, are suffering all the miseries of famine and disease. Even those who have oats cannot convert it to use for want of a sufficiency of mills to grind it. There is no appearance of the works, which were presented at the Extraordinary Sessions, being commenced. From all these causes, the peoples' minds are alarmed beyond calculation. The calamity has been so great that nothing but giving employment on the most expensive scale, and keeping an abundant supply of provisions in the country, could prevent unusual famine and all its accompanying horrors. Sanguine hopes were hitherto entertained that the government were resolved to adopt the necessary measures to prevent so dreadful a state of things. These hopes were founded partly, on the character of the several members composing the present government, and partly on the promises made by them, but alas these hopes seem now to be dissipated and a universal gloom is coming over the minds of the people which, in all probability will end in violence and plunder and universal confusion ...

(Letter dated 1 October 1846: Bernard Durcan to Henry Labouchere; Swinford DP 5916; Swords, *In Their Own Voices*, pp. 82–3)

The following was written by Friar John O'Sullivan, parish priest of Kenmare, to Charles Trevelyan on 2 December 1847.

Would to God that you could stand for one five minutes in our street, and see with what a troop of miserable, squalid, starving creatures you would be instantaneously surrounded, with tears in their eyes and with misery in their faces, imploring and beseeching you to get them a place in the work-house ... The landlords expect the Government will interfere, and the Government with greater justice say the land must support those who dwell thereon, but *vae victis* alas the poor between both ... Whatever be the cost or expense, or on whatever party it may fall, every Christian must admit, that the people must not be suffered to starve in the midst of plenty, and that the first duty of a Government is to provide for the poor under the circumstances such as they are placed ...

(Treasury Papers, Public Record Office, London; cited in Gray, *Famine, Land and Politics*, p. 284)

Historians' estimates of evictions as a consequence of the famine have differed sharply. In the nineteenth and early twentieth centuries estimates that close to a million people were dispossessed were not uncommon – Michael Davitt, writing in The Fall of Feudalism in Ireland in 1904, suggested that a wholesale system of clearances began in 1849, leading to the eviction of 195,000 families or 950,000 people. Most historians accept the police eviction returns that began in 1849, which recorded permanent evictions of 47,511 families between 1849 and 1854. Yet there has been a huge divergence in historians' analyses of court figures dealing with evictions, with estimates ranging from as little as 70,000 to as much as half a million. Recently, Tim O'Neill noted that while most historians have examined the same parliamentary returns of evictions brought before the courts in the period 1846–9, they have interpreted them in very different ways. (In every action taken to evict, a process was entered in the appropriate court office.) Many scholars estimated evictions on the basis of eviction processes entered rather than those served. O'Neill has argued that this general agreement grossly underestimates the numbers affected by court proceedings and the real impact of the famine on the rate of evictions. In trying to estimate how many tenants were ejected and then readmitted, historians have generally opted for an estimate of 20 per cent of eviction proceedings brought or entered as being a reasonable estimate. O'Neill suggests looking at the number of processes served, which, between 1846 and 1849, gives an estimate of 140,835 families and suggests that 97,248 families were evicted in the years 1846–8. To this he adds the 47,511 families recorded by the police as being permanently evicted in the period 1849–54, giving a total of 144,759 families evicted. Although it is impossible to record an accurate figure, O'Neill's examination of complex legal processes, which makes allowances for proceedings which were struck out or never pursued, has led him to the conclusion that the true number of evictions is close to 580,000 people, a higher figure than that arrived at by those who have ignored court statistics and estimated evictions. The courts statistics indicate that evictions peaked in 1848. Given that by 1848–9 the population had been further reduced by emigration and starvation, evictions would have had an even greater impact on the farming community which survived the earlier famine years.

Ejectments Brought and Served, 1846–49

Court	1846 Brought	1846 Served	1847 Brought	1847 Served	1848 Brought	1848 Served	1849 Brought	1849 Served
Queen's Bench	877	6,251	2,992	18,023	2,823	26,865	1,003	9,168
Common Pleas	62	598	115	2,154	104	1,422	21	226
Exchequer	562	3,947	1,117	9,289	1,288	9,261	391	1,858
Assistant Barristers	3,170	8,908	7,628	21,766	12,382	31,351	3,294	8,581
Total	**4,671**	**19,704**	**10,862**	**51,232**	**16,597**	**69,899**	**4,709**	**19,833**

(*Abstract of Returns Relating to Ejectments, Ireland Parliamentary Papers* 1849 (315), xlix, p.7;

Tim O'Neill, 'Famine Evictions', in Carla King (ed.), *Famine, Land and Culture in Ireland*

(Dublin, 2000))

Extract from rental of the Earl of Midleton's estate in Counties Cork and Waterford, 7 August 1847.

No. 368	Received notice to quit
No. 369	Two of the tenants, Jeremiah and John Hegarty, sent to Canada, their portion of arrear will be lost.
No. 370	Tenant dead; notice to quit given to his widow
No. 372	Tenant removed; arrear lost
No. 373	Arrear lost; tenant sent to Canada
Nos. 375, 376 & 377	Notices to quit at next March given
No. 379	Arrear lost; tenant sent to Canada
No. 380	Received notice to quit at March next
No. 381	Arrear lost; tenant sent to Canada
No. 382 & 384	Notices to quit at March next given in these two numbers
No. 386	To be removed by ejectment
No. 387	Arrear lost; tenant sent to Canada
Nos. 390 & 391	Notices given to quit at March next
No. 394	Notice given to quit at March next
No. 395	Arrear lost; tenant removed
No. 396	Tenant dead; notice to quit given to his widow
No. 397	Arrear lost; tenant and family sent to Canada

(NAI, 978/2/3/2/1)

James Hack Tuke's writings on the human consequences of evictions by Mayo propri-
etors had caused considerable public controversy by the end of 1847. Tuke was a
Quaker from Yorkshire in England.

Although so much has already been said about evictions, I can hardly omit to mention one instance which occurred very shortly before my visit, and which presents a striking instance of the cruelty connected with that system of extermination which many Irish landlords think themselves justified as adopting. The extreme western portion of Erris is a narrow promontory called the 'Inner Mullet'. Upon this wretched promontory, a proprietor named Walsh, residing in another part of the country, has an estate from which he was desirous of ejecting a number of tenants by the usual summary process of unroofing and eviction. As no less than 140 families were to be turned out and cast forth to beg or perish, for the poorhouse was fifty miles distant and could not have contained them, it was natural to expect some resistance from persons with such prospects.

The landlord, therefore, summons the sheriff to his assistance – the stipendiary magistrate is requested to call out the police; but a maddened tenantry may overcome a handful of police. Fifty soldiers, therefore, headed by the commanding officer of the district, are added to the force. It is thought the 'kindest' way to prevent bloodshed, by showing a superior power. Arrived at the scene of action, the troops are stationed in a reserve behind a hill, and the landlord and sheriff, protected by forty policemen, proceeded to announce their errand. The tenants are commanded to quit – they are told that their landlord forgives all arrears, on condition of their quietly giving up possession of their hovels and holdings, and leaving their crops should they have any. But the poor tenants, knowing the consequence of this, remonstrate – entreat, at least for time – but all in vain; the decree has passed.

The policemen are commanded to do their duty. Reluctantly indeed they proceed, armed with bayonet and musket, to throw out the miserable furniture; dirty time-worn stools and bed-frame, if any, ragged cover-lid, iron pot; all must be cast out and the very roof of the hovel itself thrown down. But, the tenants make some show of resistance – for these hovels have been built by themselves or their forefathers who have resided in them for generations past – seem inclined to dispute with the bayonets of the police, for they know truly that, when their hovels are demolished, the nearest ditch must be their dwelling, and that thus exposed, death could not fail to be the lot of some of their wives and little ones. But the signal is given to the soldiers, and overawed by the unexpected sight, the tenants are compelled to submit, and in despair and dismay to see the ruthless work proceed.

Six or seven hundred persons were here evicted; young and old, mother and babe were alike cast forth, without shelter and without the means of subsistence! A favoured few were allowed to remain, on condition that in six months they would voluntarily depart. 'A fountain of ink (as one of them has said) would not write half our misfortunes'; and I feel that it is utterly beyond my power to describe the full misery of this and similar scenes. At a dinner party that evening, the landlord, as I was told by one of the party, boasted that this was the first time he had seen the estate or visited the tenants. Truly, their first impression of landlordism was not likely to be a very favourable one!

(James Hack Tuke, A Visit to Connaught in the Autumn of 1847; a Letter Addressed to the Central Relief Committee of the Society of Friends (Dublin, 1847), pp. 24–26)

The Illustrated London News frequently commented on the evictions of peasantry in Ireland, particularly in the latter stages of the famine, seeing them as a necessary evil.

A vast social change is gradually taking place in Ireland. The increase of emigration on the part of the bulk of the small capitalists, and the eject-ment, by wholesale, of the wretched cottiers, will, in the course of a short time, render quite inappropriate for its new condition the old cry of a re-dundant population. But this social revolution, however necessary it may be, is accompanied by an amount of human misery that is absolutely ap-palling. The *Tipperary Vindicator* thus portrays the state of the country:

The work of undermining the population is going on stealthily, but steadily. Each succeeding day witnesses its devastation – more terrible than the simoon, and more deadly than the plague. We do not say that there exists a conspiracy to uproot the 'mere Irish'; but we do aver, that the fearful system of wholesale ejectment, of which we daily hear, and which we daily behold, is a mockery of the eternal laws of God – a flagrant outrage on the principles of nature. Whole districts are cleared. Not a roof-tree is to be seen where the happy cottage of the labourer or the snug home-stead of the farmer at no distant day cheered the landscape.

The ditch side, the dripping rain, and the cold sleet are the covering of the wretched outcast the moment the cabin is tumbled over him; for who dare give him shelter or protection from the 'pelting of the pitiless storm'? Who has the temerity to afford him the ordinary rites of hospitality, when the warrant has been signed for his extinction?

There are vast tracts of the most fertile land in the world in this noble country now thrown out of tillage. No spade, no plough goes near them. There are no symptoms of life within their borders, no more than if they were situated in the midst of the Great Desert – no more than if they were cursed by the Creator with the blight of barrenness. Those who laboured to bring those tracts to the condition in which they are – capable of raising produce of any description – are hunted like wolves, or they perish without a murmur. The tongue refuses to utter their most deplorable – their un-heard-of sufferings. The agonies endured by the 'mere Irish' in this day of their unparalleled affliction are far more poignant than the imagination could conceive, or the pencil of a Rembrandt picture. We do not exaggerate; the state of things is absolutely fearful; a demon, with all the vindictive passions by which alone a demon could be influenced, is let loose and menaces destruction. Additional sharpness, too, is imparted to his appetite. Christmas was accustomed to come with many healing balsams, sufficient to remove irritation, if not to staunch wounds; but its place is usurped by other and far different qualifications. The howl of misery has succeeded the merry carol which used to usher in the season; no hope is felt that the end will soon be put to this state of wretchedness. The torpor and apathy which have seized on the masses are only surpassed by the atrocities perpetrated by those who set the dictates of humanity and the decrees of the Almighty at equal defiance.

(*Illustrated London News* (16 December 1848))

... The truth is that these evictions ... are not merely a legal but a natural process; and however much we may deplore the misery from which they spring, and which they so dreadfully aggravate, we cannot compel the Irish proprietors to continue in their miserable holdings the wretched swarms of people who pay no rent, and who prevent the improvement of property so long as they remain upon it ... it sounds very well to English ears to preach forbearance and generosity to the landowners. But it should be remembered that few of them have it in their power to be merciful or generous to their poorer tenantry ... They are themselves engaged in a life and death struggle with their creditors. Moreover, the greater number of the depopulators are mere agents for absent landlords or for the law-receivers under the courts acting for creditors ... [T]hose landlords who have yet some voice in the management of their estates ... think themselves justified – most of them, indeed, are compelled by the overwhelming pressure of their own difficulties – to follow the example [of the receivers for estates under Court of Chancery jurisdiction].

(*Illustrated London News* (21 October 1849))

Testimonies collected by the Irish Folklore Commission in the 1930s and 1940s contain interesting observations on the theme of forced eviction, not necessarily just by land-lords.

Ned Buckley, Knocknagree, County Cork

In my young day I used to hear old people discuss the awful cruelty prac-tised by farmers who were fairly well-off against the poorer and less com-fortable neighbours. The people who were old when I was young, I'm 66, were never tired of discussing how some of those, taking advantage of the poverty of their neighbours, used to offer the rent of their farms to the land-lord, the rent which the owners could not pay, and grab their farms adding some to their own farms.

I used to hear how back in Bawnard on the Kerry side of the Blackwater, how old Johnny Mahony paid the rent and grabbed the farm of old Owen Casey, without poor Casey knowing a bit about it. Mahony just paid the year's rent, got a receipt for same and came home, with his own hands doing the bailiff and evicted himself, turned out poor Casey and his wife from their house and home. Poor Casey had the spring work done, the oats and potatoes set, but had to leave them all. The garden grew and the time came when the spuds were fit to dig and the woman who helped to get them, Mrs Casey, came one morning to dig her breakfast of the praties she herself and her husband had sown, but old Mahony came at her and broke her spade and broke her hand and sent her off without anything for the breakfast. The old people used tell how no luck ever attended the Mahony family after and now there's no one belonging to them in the place, and they pointed out a lot more people who came by farms in this way whose families melted away and of whom there is no trace to this day. Several peo-ple would be glad if the Famine times were altogether forgotten so that the cruel doings of their forbears would not be again renewed and talked about by neighbours.

(IFC 1071: 77-154; Cathal Póirtéir, Famine Echoes (Dublin, 1995), pp. 217–18)

Michael Corduff, The Lodge, Westport, Ballina, County Mayo

During the time of the Great Famine, a century ago, there lived in the town-land of Kilgalligan a landlord's bailiff who was known by the name of Jack

Mor a Raighaillaigh. Like his neighbours, he was a small farmer and used to have some tillage. Like most of the bailiffs of his kind he was an oppressor and with sternness he dominated and exercised his despotism over the community amongst whom he lived. People speak in scathing terms of landlords in the past and not without much justification in many cases, but my opinion is that they were not half as bad as the native hirelings in their employment and Jack Mor it appears was one of the worst of his ilk.

There was a widow in the village whose husband had only died recently and she had two little orphan boys. The father had died recently of starvation, for in those days the primitive and scanty nature of the peoples' food was unable to sustain life in numerous cases for long. The two children were one day discovered by the bailiff on his land searching for potatoes in the soil called 'pratai romhair' [digging potatoes]. These were potatoes which having escaped the digger the previous season, grew up again, but they were invariably of very inferior quality and were only fed to animals. Of course, in the time of the Famine people would eat almost anything and these two children were out to procure the makings of a 'cast' to roast in the ashes for themselves, but the merciless bailiff soon put an end to their operations. He seized the two children and brought them to his house, and secured them to the cow's stake at the end of the kitchen, he then returned to his work in the field, having told his wife not to release the children until he would come back to his midday meal. She was making stirabout and it is said she gave some of it to eat to the two children in the absence of the husband. The plight of the two children owing to their cruel captivity and fear was extremely sad. Their mother came to the house of their confinement and begged their release, but the woman of the house who was kind and charitable, and the direct opposite of her haughty and wicked husband, was afraid to incur her husband's displeasure by letting the children go. The mother then went to the field where the bailiff was working and begged for the children's release. Instead of showing any sympathy or mercy for the poor woman in her woe, he merely threatened to do the same to herself and that there was further punishment awaiting the two boys on his return to the house.

She told him to do his wickedest and perhaps he would repent of his cruelty sooner than he expected. On reaching home she went through all of the prescribed formalities of the widow's curse and on her knees she exercised her incantations for evil on her enemy, the bailiff. Before the appointed time for returning to his dinner Jack Mor was seized with a severe pain in his side, so he had to return to the house and lie on his bed writhing in agony.

In the consternation which followed in the household consequent on the suffering of the man of the house, no attention was paid to the chained boys and one of them managed to release himself and his brother. When leaving the house one of them said to the other, 'Now, thank God, we are free, but neither God, man nor devil will ever release you.'

The suffering man sent for the woman whom he had injured and begged her forgiveness, but she merely said she would leave him to God to deal with, as he was only reaping the fruits of his bad deeds. He died in a few hours. Many misdeeds could be quoted against him. He even used to intercept the fishermen and compel them to hand over to him any quantity of fish which he demanded.

(IFC 1072: 1–64, Póirtéir, *Famine Echoes*, pp. 223–5)

Particularly active in the provision of relief by way of private charity was the Society of Friends (Quakers), who in November 1846 established a Central Relief Committee that co-ordinated relief policies between themselves, their co-religionists in Ireland and London-based Quakers. Although the number of Quakers in Ireland was small, members such as the Bewley and Pim families were prosperous and enterprising business people; their accounts of famine relief are marked by huge sympathy with the plight of the victims but also an insistence on the need for industriousness and self-reliance. The appearance of famine also prompted the re-establishment of the Irish Relief Association, based in Dublin, and the General Central Relief Committee. Other important bodies included the British Relief Association, the Ladies' Work Association and various American relief committees.

Principal British and Irish Non-governmental Relief Committees and Funds, 1845–51.

	£
Local contributions to attract matching governmental funds, 1846	104,690
Local contributions to attract matching governmental funds, 1847	199,569
British Relief Association, total received:	470,041
five-sixths for Ireland [one-sixth for Scotland]	391,701
Central Relief Committee for All Ireland, College Green, Dublin: £83,935, less £20,190 from British Relief Association	63,745
Irish Relief Association, Sackville Street, Dublin	42,446
Relief Committee of the Society of Friends, Dublin: £198,314, less amount received from the Committee of Friends in London and interest £39,250	159,064
Society of Friends, London	42,906
Indian Relief Fund	13,920
National Club, London	19,930
Wesleyan Methodist Relief Fund	20,057
Irish Evangelical Society, London	9,264
Baptists' Relief Fund, London	6,142
Ladies' Irish Clothing Society, London: £9,533, less amount received from the British Association £5,325	4,208
Ladies' Relief Association for Ireland: £19,584, less amount received from the British Association £7,659	11,925

Ladies' Industrial Society for the Encouragement of Labour among the Peasantry	25,752
Belfast Ladies' Association for the Relief of Irish Distress	2,617
Belfast Ladies' Industrial Association for Connaught	4,616
Two Belfast collections	10,000
Estimates of emigrants' remittances	
1848	460,180
1849	540,619
1850	957,087
1851	990,811

(Tim O'Neill, 'The Charities and Famine in Mid-nineteenth Century Ireland', in Jacqueline Hill and Colm Lennon (eds.), *Luxury and Austerity, Historical Studies XXI* (Dublin, 1999), pp. 137–64)

Extracts from Minute Book No. 1 of the Central Relief Committee of the Society of Friends.

9 April 1847

The notice of the meeting has been called to the extreme want of proper clothing which prevails among the labourers in some of the districts which have been visited by Friends who are present and considering the very important bearing which the supply of clothing has upon the preservation of life and health, we think that a portion of the funds may be legitimately and properly applied to this object. We have been painfully affected by the accounts received of the circumstances of distress into which many small tradesmen and artisans have fallen in consequence of the almost entire suspension of their general occupations arising from the general impoverishment of the country, and although cases of this kind appear to call for a more than common degree of circumspection in the administration of relief, we think that many instances may occur in which some assistance to persons in these classes may be very properly given. We also consider that the many children who have recently become orphans by the extended prevalence of famine and disease, have a very peculiar claim upon our sympathy and care. It is obvious that from the widespread existence of extreme weakness and disease, there will be numerous calls for the exercise of pecuniary aid towards this class of community. In connection with the present calamities of Ireland this meeting has also had its attention turned to the consideration of several important subjects connected with the social interests of the country, amongst which may be mentioned the improvement of the fisheries, the encouragement of the cultivation of flax and of the domestic manufacture of articles adapted for the use of the peasantry. And the promotion of the industrial education of the young, particularly of the large numbers of children assembled in the union poor houses; for while all these objects appear to the meeting to be of great importance to the well being of Ireland and to be highly deserving of support and encouragement, we are nevertheless of the judgement that so long as serious demands in connection with the great and primary object for which the funds at our disposal have been raised, namely, that of feeding the hungry and clothing the naked, who are suffering under the effects of the present visitation remain unsatisfied, we should not be justified, except with a view to the immediate promotion of that object in furnishing pecuniary aid to measures of a more general character, however great may be their interest and importance ...

11 September 1847

The distress existing in some parts of the country consequent on the cessation of the temporary measures of relief having been brought before us by letters from Cork and other parts including letters from the Waterford Committee respecting clothing and from the Limerick Committee for their large distribution of the means placed at their disposal by William Rathbone of Liverpool; and the subjects being deliberated on at considerable length and as it appears that our funds are wholly inadequate to warrant us in offering any comprehensive system of relief to those classes for whom a provision is made by law, and being apprehensive that temporary assistance would retard the carrying of the new Poor Law into effective operation, it is the opinion of this committee that it is expedient very much at present very much to discontinue our issues of food and that it is desirable to retain the means remaining at our disposal for the assistance of those classes of distressed persons whom the stringency of legal measures and relief must exclude from care – for the supplying of nourishing food to the sick and convalescent in cases of inadequate hospital accommodation, and for the promotion of industrial objects and other undertakings having a bearing on the permanent improvement of the conditions of the people. It is also our opinion that it would be desirable to allocate a considerable portion of our funds for the purpose of supplying clothing to the destitute under such checks as may be practicable against the clothes being misapplied ...

13 November 1847

An application having been received from Maurice O'Connell MP of Derrynane Abbey, County Kerry, for a grant of money to enable him to purchase boats, gear and nets for the purpose of encouraging the fishing in his locality, thus affording the means of support to the numerous unemployed fishermen and their families who are at present in a most helpless state of want and misery – on the terms that he should employ the means placed at his disposal by this committee in a regular undertaking expected to be remunerative and that neither money nor gear should be given without the repayment of same having first been arranged for and secured. That he should give his promissory note or notes for the amount lent him by this committee payable at nine or twelve months, and that the sum he should wish to be placed at his disposal should be from £200 to £300. This committee agrees to the proposition made by Maurice O'Connell MP and will place the sum he names, say, £300 at his disposal – on the terms of security stated and the secretaries are requested to draw up a memorandum of arrangement as to the mode the money should be expended and the manner in which he would wish to receive it ...

(NAI, SFFP, 2/506/2)

It was probably the case that most Quakers working to alleviate suffering were not driven by a desire to proselytise, though there is evidence that some of this occurred. This report was sent to the Quakers by Emily and Rebecca Irwin, from Boyle, County Roscommon, on 7 October 1847.

It is well known to all who have taken an interest in the moral and religious condition of Ireland, that the work of education has, in large districts of the country, hardly been commenced. Our school, within the demesne of Camlin, supported partly by the London Ladies Hibernian Schools Society and partly by private contributions, is the only school of any kind in a circle of miles around this, except the national schools, and these are entirely under the superintendence and patronage of Roman Catholic priests and taught by Roman Catholic teachers. The Scriptures are completely excluded from these, for popery cannot tolerate the light of the truth as it is in Jesus, and even the secular instruction given in them is of a very inferior description. The teachers being all males, nothing whatever is done in the way of instructing the girls in needlework, knitting, etc., so that they grow up ignorant of all those arts of industry and meekness that make the houses of the English lower classes so infinitely superior to ours.

Hitherto the priests made so successful a resistance to our Bible training that our present school house was sufficiently large for all the children we could induce to attend. The district being one of the most popish in all Ireland, every parent who had the hardihood to send his children did so in defiance of all the obstacles that Romish priests and popery could throw in his way and these are neither few nor easily surmounted. But the troubles of the last year have wrought a wonderful change. The people have greatly lost faith in their own church and clergy and are now ready to receive sounder instruction for themselves and their children. Such has been the anxiety for admission to the school that we have taken in a considerably larger number than our school room would conveniently accommodate and we are daily under the painful necessity of rejecting fresh applications. We know how ready popery will be to reassert its former influence over such as may outlive their hard times and are therefore all the more anxious to work while we have an open door. If the necessity was equally great before, the opportunity was certainly not so tempting. Consequently we have resolved to lay our case before some of our Christian friends, hoping for their co-operation in the work of collecting funds for the creation of a new house capable of containing both our male and female classes ...

(NAI SFFP 2/506/21; Swords, *In Their Own Words*, pp. 230–31)

Extract from the proceedings of the first meeting of the General Central Relief Committee for All Ireland, 31 December 1846.

Resolved that, thoroughly acquainted as we are with the state of Ireland, we do feel it a solemn duty to warn the friends of humanity of the awful deficiency of food for subsistence in this country, for even a short period, the deficiency being so great as to threaten with certain death, hundreds of thousands of our fellow creatures; and unless the most active, prompt and persevering exertions be made to augment in an almost indescribable degree, the quantity of food at present in Ireland, famine and pestilence will desolate the land.

Resolved – that in calling on the humane and charitable to assist us in this great national undertaking, we solemnly pledge ourselves that the most searching enquiry shall precede relief in every instance, so that the really destitute shall alone receive succour from this committee.

(NAI, SFFP 2/507/3, *Report of the Proceedings of the General Central Relief Committee for All Ireland from Its Formation on 29th December 1846 to the 31st December, 1847* (Dublin, 1848))

Report of the proceedings of the 18 January 1847 meeting of the Irish Relief Association.

The transmission of provision to the most distressed districts has been the great object, to which from the beginning, the attention of the committee has been directed. The employment of the peasantry in various public works has given them, in some degree, the means of purchasing food, when it is to be had; but, in many instances, the supply of provisions is either wholly inadequate to the demand, or they are sold at such a price to place it beyond the power of the people, even with an increased rate of wages, to purchase a sufficient quantity for the support of themselves and their families. There are also many thousands in the suffering districts, who from infirm health and other causes, cannot obtain employment, and to whom food must be distributed gratuitously. In order to overcome, if possible, this difficulty, it has been the object of the Committee to sell food at a reduced price to those who are able to purchase; and, in particular instances, to give gratuitously, through the agency of persons residing on the spot, in whom confidence can be placed. With the view of carrying out this principle, two cargoes of meal were sent to districts in the Counties of Donegal and Mayo, of the extreme destitution of which, alarming accounts had reached the committee. Being unable for some time to obtain a steamer for the purpose, they were compelled to resort, as a matter of necessity, to sailing vessels, which, they are happy to say, reached their destination some weeks ago. The cost of these cargoes was £1,658 14s. 6d. which with the expense of freight etc., amounting to £137 6s. 8d., makes in all £1,796 0s. 11d.

The Committee have paid the freight of 2 sailing vessels, destined for Gweedore and Dingle and chartered by two private individuals, with provisions for the poor of those districts, and it is gratifying to be able to add that they have also reached their destination. The expense incurred by this arrangement amounted to £86 0s. 3d. The Committee have at length succeeded in obtaining a steamer, of 300 tons burthen, which has been loaded in Liverpool with about 250 tons of corn and meal in addition to which the Society of Friends and the Relief Committee of St. Jude's, Liverpool, have shipped fifty tons of various articles for making soup, and it has been dispatched with orders to make deposits at various places along the western coast, to be lodged in stores and sold at reduced prices. The purchase of this cargo amounts to £4,570, exclusive of the hire of the vessel, and various contingent expenses not yet ascertained, which will amount to a considerable sum ...

(NAI, SFFP 2/507/3, Distress in Ireland: Irish Relief Association for the Destitute Peasantry, being a Re-organisation of the Association Formed during the Period of Famine in the West of Ireland in 1831 (Dublin, 1847))

Queen Victoria's letter to the Archbishop of Canterbury asking for a collection in aid of the relief of famine victims in Ireland and some parts of Scotland requesting that an appeal should be read in each church announcing that a collection for famine relief would be made over the following few weeks. Following this a proclamation announced that 24 March 1847 would be appointed as a day of fasting, also in order to raise funds. Within a few weeks, £171,533 was raised as a result of the letter and the fast.

Victoria Regina,

Most Reverend Father in God, our right trusty and right entirely beloved councillor, we greet you well. Whereas a large portion of the population of Ireland, and in some districts of Scotland, is suffering severe distress, owing to the failure of the ordinary supplies of food; and whereas many of our subjects have entered into voluntary subscriptions for their relief, and have at the same time humbly prayed to us to issue our Royal Letters, directed to the Lord Archbishop of Canterbury and the Lord Archbishop of York, authorising them to promote contributions within their respective provinces for the same benevolent purpose.

We, taking the premises into our Royal consideration, and being always ready to give the best encouragement and countenance to such humane and charitable undertakings, are graciously pleased to condescend to their request; and we do hereby direct that these letters be by you communicated to the several Suffragen Bishops within your province, expressly requiring them to take care that publication be made hereof on such Sunday in the present or ensuing month, and in such places within the respective dioceses, as the said Bishops shall appoint; and that upon this occasion the ministers in each parish do effectually excite their parishioners to a liberal contribution, which shall be collected the week following at their respective dwellings by the churchwardens or overseers of the poor in each parish; and the ministers of the several parishes are to cause the sums so collected to be paid immediately into the hands of the Bank of England, to be accounted for by them, and applied to the carrying on and promoting the above mentioned good designs.

And so we bid you very heartily farewell.

Given at the Court at St James, the 13th day of January 1847, in the tenth year of our reign.

(The Times, 22 January 1847)

Extract from a lecture by John Hughes, Bishop of New York, on the Irish famine, delivered in New York in March 1847.

America offers her, not a sympathy of mere sentiment and feeling but that substantial sympathy which her sympathy requires. When the first news of your benevolence and of your efforts shall have been wafted across the ocean, it will sound as sweetly in her agonised ear as the voice of angels whispering hope. It will cause her famine-shrunken heart to expand again to its native fullness, whilst from day to day the western breezes will convey her echoes of the rising song, the swelling chorus, the universal outburst, in short, of American sympathy. The bread with which your ships are freighted will arrive too late for many a suffering child of hers; but the news that it is coming, will perchance reach the peasant's cabin, in the final hour of his mortal agony. Unable to speak, gratitude will wreath, in feeble smile, for the last time, his pinched and pallid countenance. It is the smile of hope as well as gratitude; hope, not for himself, it comes too late for that, but for his pale wife and famished little ones. He will recline his head more calmly, he will die with yet more subdued resignation, having discovered at the close of his life that truth which the whole training and experience of his hard lot in this world had almost taught him to deny, namely, that there is humanity in mankind, and that its blessings are about to reach even his cabin, from a quarter in which he had no other claim, than that of his misfortune ...

(John Hughes, DD, Bishop of New York, *A Lecture on the Antecedent Causes of the Irish Famine in 1847, Delivered under the Auspices of the General Committee for the Relief of the Suffering Poor of Ireland* (New York, 1847))

Famine Relief Funds Raised in American Cities

	$
New York	170,150
Newark and State of New Jersey	35,000
Boston	45,000
Baltimore	40,000
Philadelphia	50,000
New Orleans	25,000
Albany	25,000
Washington	5,000
Total	**395,150**

(*Dublin Evening Mail*, 17 April 1847; Christine Kinealy, *This Great Calamity: The Irish Famine 1845–52* (Dublin, 1994), p. 164)

The Atlantic crossing, undertaken by so many Irish in the years 1847 to 1852, was primarily to North America. Emigration from Ireland was by no means a new phenomenon, but the psychological and emotive context in which it occurred after 1847 certainly became more pronounced and, undoubtedly, more harrowing. Another notable feature of famine emigration was that, rather than making the traditional summer departures, many emigrated in both autumn and winter. The cold weather would undoubtedly have exacerbated travelling conditions, along with fever, starvation and lack of clothing and sanitation on board, as would the fact that most people were seeking the cheapest possible means of transport. Many, for example, would have had to have made their way to Liverpool, to sail from there rather than from Dublin; Canada was also a cheaper destination than the United States, but with far less rigid controls on shipboard conditions. There was certain pressure on the government to introduce assisted emigration as part of famine relief, but the cost – not to mention the responsibility – were thought to be prohibitive, with an exception made for certain orphaned children. Some landlords assisted emigration in an individual capacity. Despite certain unique characteristics of famine emigration, many historians contend that it represented a continuous process, given that emigration was already rising rapidly in the years before the famine.

A letter from James Prendergast of Milltown, County Kerry to three of his children at their new home in Boston in November 1846. The original Prendergast famine letters are preserved in the archives at Burns College, Boston. Prendergast, who could write only his signature, dictated the letters to a local scrivener.

My dear children,

On the 11th of August last I wrote in reply to your letter of the 16th of July, thanking you for your remittance which was a relief received most kindly. Since that time we were most anxiously expecting an answer from ye. At last our patience was worn out and we became really alarmed, not for any disappointment of our own, but lest any disaster should befall either of you and cause this unusual delay. We are now old and must of course be near our dissolution, and we would descend quietly to the grave if we knew that ye were well. John Payne arrived here some time since, he said ye were well and that he heard Tom [a son] was married, but could not say it absolutely. Therefore, my dear children, we entreat you to write on receipt of this and ease our troubled minds. Say, if either of the boys married, if so may God bless them. The state of this country is almost beyond description. Nothing to be seen in all quarters but distress and destitution. Famine and starvation threatening everywhere unless God mercifully send some foreign aid. Last year was a year of abundance and plenty when compared with the present. This year all the potato crop was lost, the best farmer here is as short of them as the poorer class. Potatoes are seldom in the market, and the few that then come are bought by the rich as a rarity at the rate of from £8 to £12 for stone ... The supply of the country it is dreaded will soon be exhausted unless supplies are brought in from abroad. The grain crop of this country fell very short this year. The last remittance ye sent is out long since and we are considerably in debt. Therefore, if ye can assist us as usual do not delay your usual relief. The pawn offices are so stacked with goods that 10 shillings could scarcely be raised on the value of five pounds. Let Con know that his brother is in his usual place ... I remain affectionately,

Your Father,

James Prendergast.

(Michael Costello (ed.), *The Famine in Kerry* (Kerry, 1997))

The Times leading article of 17 September 1847, dealing with the exodus to Canada.

The Great Irish Famine and pestilence will have a place in that melancholy series of similar calamities to which historians and poets have contributed so many harrowing details and touching expressions. Did Ireland possess a writer endowed with the laborious truth of Thucydides, the graceful felicity of Virgil, or the happy invention of De Foe, the events of this miserable year might be quoted by the scholars for ages to come together with the sufferings of the pent-up multitudes of Athens, the distempered plains of Northern Italy, or the hideous ravages of our own Great Plague. But time is ever improving on the past. There is one horrible feature of the recent, not to say the present visitation which is entirely new. The fact of more than a hundred thousand souls flying from the very midst of the calamity across a great ocean to the new world, crowding into insufficient vessels, scrambling for a footing on a deck and a berth in a hold, committing themselves to these worse than prisons, while their frames were wasted with ill fare and their blood infected with disease. Fighting for months of unutterable wretchedness against the elements without and pestilence within, giving almost hourly victims to the deep, landing at length on shores already terrified and diseased, consigned to encampments of the dying and of the dead, spreading death wherever they roam and having no other prospect before them than a long continuance of these horrors in a still farther flight across forests and lakes under a Canadian sun and a Canadian frost – all these are circumstances beyond the experience of the Greek historian or the Latin poet and such as an Irish pestilence alone could produce.

By the end of the season there is little doubt that the immigration into Canada alone will have amounted to 100,000, nearly all from Ireland. We know the conditions in which these poor creatures embarked on their perilous adventure. They were only flying from one form of death. On the authority of the Montreal Board of Health we are enabled to state that they were allowed to ship in numbers two or three times greater than the same vessels would presumed to have carry to a United States port. The worst horrors of that slave trade which it is the boast or the ambition of this Empire to suppress, at any cost, have been re-enacted in the flight of British subjects from their native shores. In only ten of the vessels that arrived at Montreal in July, four from Cork and six from Liverpool, out of 4,427 passengers, 804 had died on the passage and 847 were sick on their arrival; that is, 847 were visibly diseased, for the result proves that a far larger number had in them the seeds of disease ...

(The Times (17 September 1847))

Certain landlords also assisted tenants to emigrate to Australia, while the government organised the settlement there of some orphaned children from Irish workhouses. The following letter was sent to Lord Monteagle, who as well as helping tenants from his own estate in Shanagolden, lobbied the government to adopt a programme of assisted emigration. This letter was printed in the form of a circular as part of the campaign to encourage emigration.

Melbourne, Port Philip

20th March, 1848

My Lord,

I, as in duty bound, feel called upon to inform your lordship how the Emigrants who obtained a passage through your lordship's intercession are situated. All the Girls are employed in the Town of Melbourne, at the rate of Twenty-five to Twenty-six pounds per annum; they are all in respectable places. Thos. Sheahan is employed in the Town adjoining, attending Bricklayers at Four Shillings and Six pence per day – John Enright on Public work, at the same rate. The general hire for Labourers of every description, my lord, is from Twenty-eight to Thirty-two pounds per annum, with board and lodgings. There is nothing in such demand in this Colony as Male and Female Servants: I was employed myself, my lord, on board the Lady Peel, by the Colonial Doctor, filling up forms of agreement between Masters and Servants, so that I had an opportunity of knowing all the particulars concerning wages, terms of employment, occupation, &c. &c.

I would mention all, but I consider your lordship will feel satisfied when you know they are all in good situations and with respectable masters and mistresses. I have seen a good deal of the Emigrants whom I knew at home, that obtained passage through your lordship's intercession, about eleven years ago, some of them live in the Town of Melbourne, and are living comfortably. Ellen Shanahan (Loughill) is married to one Rockford, in this Town, and keeps a Hotel. Maurice Connors, of Foynes, is living in this Town, and has as much money spared as exempts him from personal labour. I have heard from some more of them who live in the Country, and as far as I can learn, my lord, they are living independently. Ellen Sheahan is just going up to her brother accompanied by her first cousin, Daniel Mulcare, of Clonnlikard, himself and his brother has lived some time in this Town, and kept a Grocer's Shop. They have acted the part of a brother to me, my lord, they gave me the best of entertainment, and procured a situation for me with one Mr Ham, a Surveyor. I am going up the Country to the Avoca River to survey a Station; my wages are Twenty-one pounds for six months. Mr Hurley has sent for his nephew and his aunt, they are on their way up by this time. I expect, my lord, to be able to remit some money to your lordship in recompense for the expenses incurred on my and my sisters' account by your lordship, as well as some relief to my poor mother, brothers and sister. I hope, my lord, this humble but imperfect epistle will find your Lordship, Lady Monteagle, Mr Spring Rice, and all his family in good health. Any information I can give your lordship respecting the interior of this Country, will not be lost sight of on my part. Mr Thos. Ham, of Great Collins Street, Melbourne, would forward any commands to me, my lord, if your lordship should want any more information concerning any of the late or former Emigrants. Every thing in this Colony, my lord, is from three to four times as dear here as it is in England or Ireland, except Bread, Beef, Mutton, &c., the best of which is obtained at Three half-pence to Twopence per lb.

I am, My Lord, with profound veneration,

Your Lordship's most devoted Servant,

P. DANAHER

P.S. My Sisters also, my lord, beg leave to return their most sincere thanks to your Lordship and Lady Monteagle.

John Flanagan and Wife are both employed by a man of the name Murphy, a Brewer, about twelve miles out in the Country, wages Fifty pounds per annum.

(NLI, Monteagle Correspondence, MS 13400 (2))

In the latter stages of the famine, Irish journalists often wrote about the challenges facing Irish emigrants and commented on the best means of prospering in a foreign land.

PRACTICAL HINTS TO EMIGRANTS

As compared with the Canadas, the western portion of the United States will, for a long time, possess attractions to settlers, by reason of the land being in a cleared state by nature ... Almost all the farmers of the western states are owners of the land they cultivate. When, for £100 a man can buy, stock, and cultivate 80 acres of land, there will be found comparatively few persons to come under any obligations to pay rent to a landlord. These farmers live plainly and healthily and work with their own hands for their living ... We must, however, caution those persons who are intent on becoming rich, against proceeding to the western states. There are no rich classes there, in the sense which we regard riches in this country – there is no luxury; comfort and sufficiency are the highest conditions; but they are generally diffused amongst all classes. Labour is there the first condition of life; and industry is the lot of all men. Wealth is not idolised; but there is no degradation connected with labour; on the contrary, it is honourable, and held in general estimation. In the remote parts of America, an industrious youth may follow any occupation without being looked down upon or sustain loss of character, and he may rationally expect to raise himself in the world by his labour. This is a very different state of things from what we find in this old country, of rich and poor, fashionable and vulgar, respectable, idle, and common hard working people. In America, a man's success must altogether rest with himself – it will depend on his industry, sobriety, diligence, and virtue; and if he do not succeed, in nine cases out of ten, the cause of failure is to be found in the deficiencies of his own character.

(Dublin Weekly Register (11 November 1848))

Emigration Rates, 1847–55

1847	219,885 persons
1848	181,316
1849	218,842
1850	213,649
1851	254,537
1852	368,764
1853	192,609
1854	150,209
1855	78,854

(David Fitzpatrick, *Irish Emigration 1801–1921* (Dublin, 1984), p. 4)

Emigration to America and Canada

Year	Number
1846:	116,000
1847:	230,000
1848–50:	200,000 annually
1851:	225,000
1852–54:	195,000 annually

(Bourke, '*Visitation of God?*' p. 67)

Irish born population of England, Scotland and Wales, 1841–61

Area	No. of Irish-born Residents (nearest 1,000)	% of Population Irish-born
1841		
England and Wales	291,000	1.8
Scotland	126,000	4.8
1851		
England and Wales	520,000	2.9
Scotland	207,000	7.2
1861		
England and Wales:	602,000	3.0
Scotland	204,000	6.6

(Frank Neal, *Black '47: Britain and the Famine Irish* (London, 1998), p. 7)

The following is an extract from a book on the Irish in America, written in 1868 by the Irish MP John Francis Maguire, in which he outlines the policies adopted by New York to deal with the influx of immigrants. His decision to travel to America was prompted by both the positive and negative accounts of the experience of the Irish in America which were channelled back to Ireland; and by his desire to assess both the ability of rural immigrants to survive in highly industrialised areas and the degree of anti-British feeling among the Irish in America. The book was dedicated to William Gladstone, later the first British Prime Minister to propose a measure of Home Rule for Ireland.

Private hospitals, or poor-houses, were established by the brokers on the outskirts of New York and Brooklyn; and from the results of an inquiry instituted by the Board of Aldermen of New York in the year 1846, an idea may be formed of the treatment received by the wretched emigrants whose hard fate drove them into those institutions. The Committee discovered in one apartment, 50 feet square, 100 sick and dying emigrants lying on straw; and among them, in their midst, the bodies of two who had died four or five days before, but who had been left for that time without burial! They found, in the course of their inquiry, that decayed vegetables, bad flour and putrid meat were specially purchased and provided for the use of the strangers! Such as had strength to escape from these slaughter-houses fled from them as from a plague, and roamed through the city, exciting the compassion, perhaps the horror, of the passers-by; those who were too ill to escape had to take their chance – such chance as poisonous food, infected air, and bad treatment afforded them of ultimate recovery. Thanks to the magnitude and notoriety of the fearful abuses of the system then shown to exist, a remedy, at once comprehensive and efficacious, was adopted – not, it is true, to come into immediate operation, but to prove in course of time one of the noblest monuments of enlightened wisdom and practical philanthropy. In the preface to the published reports of the Commissioners of Emigration, from the organisation of the Commission in 1847 to 1860, the origin of the good work is thus told:

This state of things was becoming more distressing as emigration grew larger, and it even threatened danger to the public health. A number of citizens, to whose notice these facts were specially and frequently brought – to some from their connection with commerce and navigation, to others from personal sympathy with the children of the land of their own nativity – met about the close of the year 1846, or the winter of 1847, and consulted on the means of remedying these evils. They proposed and agreed upon a plan of relief, which was presented to the Legislature of the State of New York, and was passed into a law in the session of 1847. The system then recommended and adopted was that of a permanent Commission for the relief and protection of alien emigrants arriving at the port of New York, to whose aid such emigrants should be entitled for five years after their arrival, the expenses of their establishment and other relief being defrayed by a small commutative payment from each emigrant (now two dollars and a half).

Figures, however gigantic, afford but an imperfect notion of the work, the self-imposed and disinterested work of this Commission – of the good they have accomplished, and, more important still, the evil they have prevented. When it is stated that from May 1847 to the close of 1866, the number of passengers who arrived at the port of New York was 3,659,000 – about one third of whom received temporary relief from the commissioners – we may understand how wide and vast was the field of their benevolent labours ...

(John Francis Maguire, The Irish in America (London, 1868), pp. 186–7)

Number of Overseas Emigrants from Ireland Classified by Destination, 1851–1921

	United States	Canada	Australia and New Zealand	Other Overseas	Total Overseas
1851–5	740,216	104,844	53,801	2,298	901,159
1856–60	249,618	13,274	47,740	4,428	315,060
1861–70	690,845	40,079	82,917	4,741	818,582
1871–80	449,549	25,783	61,946	5,425	542,703
1881–90	626,604	44,505	55,476	7,890	734,475
1891–1900	427,301	10,648	11,448	17,885	461,282
1901–10	418,995	38,238	11,885	16,343	485,461
1911–21	191,724	36,251	17,629	9,691	355,295
1851–1921	3,794,852	313,622	342,842	62,701	4,514,017

(*Commission on Emigration and Other Population Problems* (Dublin, 1954), pp. 309–11)

Statement of the Number of Emigrants

Which have arrived at the Port of New York, for the present year [1848], from January to September, inclusive.

From:

Ireland	72,896
Germany	40,731
England	17,223
Scotland	4,974
France	2,007
Holland	1,374
Switzerland	1,243
Norway	4,206
Wales	899
West Indies	335
Spain	225
Italy	241
Sweden	113
Poland	53
Denmark	33
Portugal	35
South America	21
Russia	11
Mexico	7
Belgium	4
China	1
Total	143,632

(*Mayo Constitution* (31 October 1848))

Thomas Bouchier, from Scariff, County Clare, had farmed in Illinois for two years with his wife and four children when Vere Henry Foster visited him in 1851. Foster (1819–1900), the son of an Anglo-Irish diplomat, committed his life and finances to programmes of assisted emigration to America. He first visited Ireland in April 1847, to carry out his father's wish to assist one of their tenants in emigrating to America from the family property in County Louth. A product of the post-Enlightenment age, Foster believed in transformation through social engineering and the role of individual responsibility in bringing about change. He believed the long-term solution for Ireland was reform of the land system, but that the immediate remedy was to assist the poor to emigrate to a land of greater opportunity. In 1889 he stated that he had assisted 22,615 women to emigrate since 1847. A letter from Foster to the editor of the Irish Farmer's Gazette described Bouchier as an example of a successful emigrant.

... Indeed it is difficult to find an Irishman who is not perfectly satisfied with having emigrated to this country. Mr Bouchier has forty acres of land under cultivation, which is partly on Congress land, which he will cultivate until it shall possess an owner; and partly on a farm of forty acres, which he bought of its former occupant with buildings and fences on it, for five dollars per acre ... Mr B[ouchier] strongly dissuades any emigrant from taking a farm of uncleared land, as the process of clearing land, for a livelihood to an emigrant, wholly inexperienced, as he is, to the use of the axe in such an occupation is enough to drive him crazy. There is always plenty of cleared land to be bought from native Americans, who are seldom unready to sell – and that at very reasonable prices – to newcomers, and to proceed further west, to clear new land, at which they are expert, and to enjoy their favourite sport of hunting deer, turkeys, squirrels, and other game.

Foster received many letters from those he had helped emigrate. The following is an extract from one written from Queen Anne County, Maryland, in 1853. It is of particular interest, in that emigrants did not often communicate information on conversion to Protestantism and the behaviour of the Irish in America.

... I am sorry to say that religion and morality are at a very low ebb in this country and this is particularly the case with the children and descendants of Irishmen who generally speaking either join the creed of the majority or become infidels. There are a great many Irish both in N. Carolina and Baltimore, and tho' there are many respectable men amongst them, I am sorry to say that the generality are a set of low degraded, drunken wretches who disgrace their country by their conduct, so that the name of Irishman is often associated in the minds of Americans with everything vile and worthless ... You will perhaps consider it strange, but it is a positive fact, that such an animal as a man or a woman does not exist in this country, and the numerous cargoes of this species which we are daily receiving from Europe, become immediately transformed into gentlemen and ladies; to call them by any other name would be an unpardonable vulgarity, and this feeling extends to the most ignorant and unenlightened clodhopper I have met with ...

(Ruth-Ann Harris, 'Vere Foster's Programmes of Assisted Emigration in the Aftermath of the Irish Famine', in Patrick Sullivan (ed.), *The Meaning of the Famine; The Irish World Wide; History, Heritage, Identity*, Vol. 6 (London and Washington, 1997), pp. 172–95)

Michael Normile wrote from Hunter Valley, Australia to his father in West Clare be-
tween 1854 and 1865. His eloquent, though unschooled, letters provide a particular
insight into the personal experience of migration and the desire to keep in touch with
developments back home.

Lochinvar

April 1st 1855

My dear Father,

I am to inform you that I received your welcomed letter on the 25th March
dated January 1st, 55 which gave me and my sister an ocean of consolation to
hear that you my stepmother brothers and sisters are in good health thank
God. As for my uncles and aunts [you never mentioned a word about them but]
I hope they are in good health too – at same time, this leaves us in a perfect State
of health thanks be to our Blessed Redeemer for his goodness towards us.

I am to inform you of the present state of the country. The Climate of this
country is far different to home. The winter is coming on with us now it is
beautiful weather the same as home summer. The summer we past was
dreadful hot, the natives felt it warmer than they did, many years before. The
heat from the sun is not the worst, but hot winds blowing off the land from
the Northern Countries that lays N or NE. We had a few days of hot winds
after Christmass. I heard that some [new] people got sun struck, in fact I was
a day and I would give a mouthful of money for a mouthfull of fresh air. I
thought it was strange to see such hot weather in the month of December ... I
mean to inform you of the fertility of this country first. If a man has a farm of
land, he can do very well. He sows wheat on the month of April and it grows
first rate wheat. After cutting the wheat he ploughs it and put in a crop of Indian Corn. He has that off before he wants the soil for wheat that is two crops
in the one year. They grow two crops of potatoes in one year. All the crops
pays very well from 11 to 15 shillings per Bushel of 60 lb Corn 9 to 11 Shis. Per
Bushel. So a man having land free can live very happily. When a settler has
good crops and has the luck of getting them in his yard or Barn, he has a gold
Crop – in fact every thing he grows pays him well but they have not planty
hands to work the land ... Hay pays a man very well in this country. It is from
12 to 16 £ per ton. This corn they grow pays well for it grows very numerous.
They give it to their horses, or sells it to town people for their Horses. All
these crops I mentioned and many more besides is grown on this country

without manure. The manure of this country is if their comes rain favourable. You will get land here for sale as much as you like from a 1000 Ac. Down to 1 acre, or otherwise you will get land here your rent the same as home. There is no poorrates or taxes but your rent to pay ... A man coming to this country he is nothing but a real fool for the first year especily Irishmen, for it is all the English system they have for working. If an Irishman goes to drive horses or bullocks here after he coming out from home, he might as well go whistle a gig [jig] to a milestone as to speak to them. I seen some people in this country drive 10 horses in a Team without ever a Bridle or rane to them. But a wissper just speak to them the same as a commanding officer would to his soldiers and they would go here and there every place he wished, or even 12 bullocks they do the same. This country is populated by every class and race of people. There is Irish, English, Scotch, Chineas, Germans, Yankees Natives and Blacks – and amongst all these there is no employer so good as a native ... There is some men in this country and when they work for a week or two they go and drink their wages whilst it holds. A man having a comfortable living at home with his family Convenient to Chappel and market and a good bed to Lye on, I would advise him to stop there, for he has many ups and downs to encounter before he has a comfortable home in this country. A man convenient to mass at home and comes here goes up the country, for perhaps he would not get a place that would suit him convenient to the Towns. He wont See the Face of A Priest but once or Twice a year ... I would advise a young man or woman that has to work hard at home and has not much by it, to come here – although wages is coming down, for there is such numbers of people Emigrating to this Country from every part of the world ... I hope you will let me know how is my uncles and Aunts or did John get Married yet. I was sorry for to hear the death of Mr O'Connors: but it is all our fate to dye. It would be too long for me to mention all the neighbours one with another so they must excuse me for not writing their names here but at the same time I wish them all an ocean of happiness, for I had no bad neighbours during my time in Derry ... I must conclude by wishing you all the happiness this life can afford and eternal happiness in the next.
Believe this to be the constant prayer of your beloved son and daughter
Michl and Bridget Normile

(David Fitzpatrick, *Oceans of Consolation; Personal Accounts of Irish Migration to Australia*

(Cork, 1994) p. 7)

The culpability of the British government for the mass deaths of the Irish potato famine was debated rigorously, both during and after the famine. Particularly controversial were the government's refusal to prevent the export of domestically produced grain, its failure to prevent mass evictions and the implementation of a Poor Law system which greatly facilitated mass clearances, in particular the Poor Law Amendment Act of June 1847 which shifted the burden of providing public relief away from the British Treasury and towards Irish landlords and their tenants. Reflecting the harsh Victorian ideological currents of the day, most British press coverage of the famine was negative and unsympathetic, particularly regarding the issue of state intervention, the degree to which the famine was a natural or divinely ordained disaster, and the character of the Irish people. Notwithstanding, many newspapers also condemned Irish landlords (many of them absentee) over the manner in which they managed their estates. Nevertheless, they generally applauded the mass clearances which came about as a result of the Gregory Clause, believing it was the only way to improve the quality of Irish agriculture and offering the classic defence of the political economists. As the famine endured, certain newspapers – notably the Illustrated London News – became more sympathetic to the plight of the victims. For nationalist propagandists like John Mitchel, deaths and evictions became an effective political weapon, through which he depicted the Irish famine as a British government policy of the deliberate extermination of the Irish poorer classes. Figures for population decline and land redistribution reveal that it was the poorest class of the Irish – the cottiers – who suffered most, and that many left behind were able to profit from their demise.

For many who moralised about the famine, identifying and eradicating abuse was done, not in the context of the need to save lives, but by pronouncing on the organising principles of state policy.

It appears to us of the very first importance to all classes of Irish society to impress on them that there is nothing really so peculiar, so exceptional, in the condition which they look upon as the pit of utter despair. It is an object to impress upon all that they must do as we do here; they must be gradually assimilated to our state; they must adapt our methods; and agitate, if agitate they will, for a perfect community in our laws, as far as those laws appear to be the source of our greater prosperity. The letters and extracts from the Irish Press which we have lately given to our readers show how deeply the delusion of some great legislative panacea has taken possession of the Irish mind. The State! The State is to do everything. The labourer asks the state for national employment and national food, the landlord with equal importunity, demands a national loan. Does the state attempt this in England? But can the state anywhere make either employment, or food, or money? It cannot. It is true it may make the attempt, but it is certain to fail. It can only succeed in exercising a slight regulating power of these things when it is so fortunate as to find them ready to its hands ...

(The Times (8 September 1846))

The almost complete reliance of the Irish on a single crop gave rise to many social, economic and cultural theories about the Irish population. The following letter to the London Times encapsulated a popular view.

Sir,

The prospect of a second year's famine in Ireland is far too serious an event to be regarded as a passing emergency, or to be met by a temporary expedient. We may vote millions to alleviate the impending calamity – we may cover the nakedness of the land with cargoes of Indian corn; but when all this is done we are as far from the end of our labours as ever. The vote of this year does not diminish the chances of a famine the next – rather it increases them. And, what is worse, people seem to acquiesce in this state of things, as if there were no help for it – as if nature had fixed her irreversible decree that once in every four or five years Ireland should be laid waste by famine. To judge from the almost periodic recurrence of these visitations, and from the tone in which people speak of them, one would imagine that Ireland was some barren rock or thirsty wilderness in an inhospitable region of the globe, to which nature had denied all the genial qualities of soil and climate and which she had filled with an exuberance of population without affording them the means, or even the possibility of subsistence. One would imagine that this miserable people had neither hands to labour with, tools to till the earth with, nor grain to sow it with. Such is really the aspect in which we of this country seem to regard the inhabitants of the sister island during the period of one of their usual famines. Our sentiments towards them are simply those of pity. Oh! How shocking, we exclaim, that these poor Irish should have lost their potatoes again! Where shall we find something to feed them with? We do not think of inquiring whether or not the dependence of a whole nation upon so precarious an article of food be a necessary or an unnecessary evil, and if unnecessary, whether it ought not to be in every way denounced and discouraged. We do not think of inquiring, with Bishop Berkeley 'whose fault is it if poor Ireland still continues poor?'

Now, the best friend to the Irish would be he who could effectually persuade them that the fault lay entirely with themselves. They inhabit a country a great part of which is at least equal in fertility to our own, with more that is capable of being made so. There is no reason, except their own wilful mismanagement, why they should not grow as fine crops of wheat as are raised in the Lothians, and, after feeding themselves, export the surplus to our shores. Yet, after years of present suffering and fearful expectation, they idly and stupidly persist in staking their very existence upon a crop, the precarious nature of which is no more than a fair set off against the small amount of labour required to produce it. Without entering into the question of how far the laws and customs relating to landed property in Ireland, how far the landlords are themselves responsible for this evil, I may safely assert that the prejudices and ignorance of the Irish people are at least as inveterate and as fatal as their misgovernment and the ill example of their superiors have been culpable and injurious. Every Irishman must needs be a farmer, and work as much or little as he pleases; the idea of being a labourer, and engaging in general employment, is revolting to him. The great object of his life is to rent a miserable patch of land, to build himself a hovel, or burrow in the earth, to marry, and if possible, to live as well as his pig. The word 'improvement' is not in his vocabulary, he is content to live as his forefathers have done. With such exalted views in his mind, the first question is how to realise them and to this the potato furnishes a speedy though treacherous reply. No other article of food promises so much at so small a cost. An acre of potatoes will maintain four times as many people as an acre of wheat, while the time and labour of cultivating it are comparatively trifling. Here, then, are abundant means of gratifying his love of idleness and what he calls independence, and so long as nature bestows the years of plenty from her revolving cycle and witholds the years of famine, things go on smoothly ... I verily believe that if the potato famine in Ireland were to continue five years longer, it would prove a greater blessing to the country than any that has ever been devised by parliamentary commissions from the Union to the present time.

I am, Sir, Yours

B

(The Times (1 September, 1846))

Understandably, Irish newspapers had entirely separate ideological assumptions, as evidenced by this extract from the Cork Examiner, *written in the light of excessive mortality in Skibbereen.*

Without food or fuel, bed or bedding, whole families are shut up in naked hovels, dropping one by one into the arms of death – death, more merciful than this world or its rulers. What can private benevolence, what can private charity do to meet this dreadful case? – Nothing. It may release one from death, or two, or three; but hundreds and thousands are sunk in the profoundest depths of misery – they are wasting away in silent despair – 'dying like rotten sheep'.

Government aid can alone be effective here. A vigorous effort can alone rescue our patient, uncomplaining people from destruction. Political economy has slain enough of victims; it has raised hecatomb upon hecatomb of fathers, mothers, children, to its cruel, bloody policy – Humanity alone can save the survivors ...

(Cork Examiner (16 December 1846))

This letter to Trevelyan from Commissary-General Hewston, writing from Limerick on 30 December 1846, seems to give credence to the complaints Friar Mathew and others made about the enormous profits being made by speculators during the famine.

Last quotations from Cork: Indian corn, £17 5s. per ton, *ex* ship; Limerick: corn not in the market; Indian meal, £18 10s. to £19 per ton. Demand excessive. Looking to the quotations in the United States markets, these are really famine prices, the corn (direct consignment from the States) not standing the consignee more than £9 or £10 per ton. The commander of an American ship, the *Isabella*, lately with a distinct consignment from New York to a house in this city, makes no scruple, in his trips in the public steamers up and down the river, to speak of the enormous profits the English and Irish houses are making by their dealings with the States. One house in Cork alone, it is affirmed, will clear £40,000 by corn speculation; and the leading firm here will, I should say, go near to £80,000, as they are now weekly turning out from 700 to 900 tons of different sorts of meal ... I sometimes am inclined to think houses give large prices for cargoes imported for a market, to keep them up; it is an uncharitable thought, but really there is so much cupidity abroad, and the wretched people suffering so intensely from the high prices of food, augmented by every party through whose hands it passes before it reaches them, it is quite disheartening to look upon ...

(*Commissariat Series*, part 1, p. 439, O'Rourke, *History*, p. 171)

Irish Grain Trade During the Famine

Year	Exports (tons)	Imports (tons)
1844	424,000	30,000
1845	513,000	28,000
1846	284,000	197,000
1847	146,000	909,000
1848	314,000	439,000

(Cormac O'Gráda, *Famine 150: Commemorative Lecture Series* (Dublin, 1997), p. 146)

As well as grain exports, livestock exports continued during the famine. Cattle exports rose steadily, and the sharp decline in the figures for pig (swine) exports can be explained by the fact that pigs were fed on potatoes. There is little evidence of agitation for restrictions on exports during the famine, as it was believed such a course of action would decrease the level of food imports. Meat was not a regular part of the diet of most Irish peasant families, and even if it had been kept in the country, given the prevailing lack of purchasing power, it is unlikely it would have reached those most in need.

Return to an Order of the Honourable The House of Commons dated 12 April 1850 ; – for,
'An Account of the Number of Live Cattle Exported from Ireland to Great Britain, in each Year from 1846 to 1849, both inclusive.'
Ordered, by The House of Commons, to be Printed, 6 June 1850.

Live Stock Exported to Great Britain from Ireland

| | 1846 | 1847 | 1848 | 1849 |
	Number	Number	Number	Number
Oxen, Bulls, and Cows	186,483	189,960	196,042	201,811
Calves	6,363	9,992	7,086	9,831
Sheep and Lambs	259,257	324,179	255,682	241,061
Swine	480,827	106,407	110,787	68,053

Note. – Since the year 1825, when the trade between Great Britain and Ireland was placed under regulations, the official record of the interchange of produce and manufactures between the two countries (except in so far as the article of corn is concerned) has of necessity been discontinued. The foregoing Return, therefore, has been framed from non-official documents, collected at the ports of exportation, and consisting chiefly of printed market and shipping reports.
Office of the Inspector-General of Imports and Exports
William Irving, Custom House, London, 27 May 1850

(BPP (8) *Reports of the Relief Commissioners, 1846–53*, p. 23)

Issac Butt, founder of the Irish Home Government Association in 1870, took issue with the contemporary approach to the question of state responsibility and intervention.

What can be more absurd, what can be more wicked, than for men professing attachment to an imperial constitution to answer claims now put forward for state assistance to the unprecedented necessities of Ireland, by talking of Ireland being a drain upon the English treasury? The exchequer is the exchequer of the United Kingdom ... If the Union be not a mockery, there exists no such thing as an English treasury ... How are these expectations to be realized, how are these pledges to be fulfilled, if the partnership is only to be one of loss and never of profit to us? if, bearing our share of all imperial burdens – when calamity falls upon us we are to be told that we then recover our separate existence as a nation, just so far as to disentitle us to the state assistance which any portion of a nation visited with such a calamity has a right to expect from the governing power? If Cornwall had been visited with the same scenes that have desolated Cork, would similar arguments have been used?

(Dublin University Magazine, XXIX (April 1847), p. 514)

The Catholic Bishop of New York, in making an appeal for charitable donations, also took the opportunity to reflect on the causes of the famine.

... the newspapers tell us that this calamity has been produced by the failure of the potato crop; but this ought not to be a sufficient cause of so frightful a consequence: the potato is but one species of the endless variety of food which the Almighty has provided for the sustenance of his creatures; and why is it that the life or death of the great body of any nation should be so little regarded as to be left dependent on the capricious growth of a single root? Many essays will be published; many eloquent speeches pronounced; much precious time unprofitably employed, by the state economists of Great Britain, assigning the causes of the scourge which now threatens to depopulate Ireland ... Some will say that it is the cruelty of unfeeling and rapacious landlords; others will have it, that it is the improvident and indolent character of the people themselves; others, still, will say that it is owing to the poverty of the country, the want of capital, the general ignorance of the people, and especially, their ignorance in reference to the improved science of agriculture. I shall not question the truth or the fallacy of any of these theories; admitting that all, if you will, to contain each more or less of truth, they yet do not explain the famine which they are cited to account for. They are themselves to be accounted for, rather as the effects of other causes, than as the real cause of effects, such as we now witness and deplore ... If the attempt, then, be not considered too bold, I shall endeavour to lay before you a brief outline of the primary, original causes, which, by the action and reaction of secondary and intermediate agencies, have produced the rapacity of landlords, the poverty of the country, the imputed want of industry among its people and the other causes to which the present calamity will be ascribed by British statesmen. I shall designate 3 causes by 3 titles: First, incompleteness of conquest; second, bad government; third; a defective or vicious system of social economy ...

(John Hughes, *A Lecture on the Antecedent Causes of the Irish Famine in 1847* (New York, 1847))

A common British view was that during a time of great commercial pressure they had consented to significant monetary sacrifice for the sake of Ireland.

... If Ireland has offered to the world the spectacle of a gigantic misery, England has also offered to the world the spectacle of an unparalleled effort to relieve and to remove it. If the splendour of our benevolence has not kept pace with the hideousness of her misery, it has not been from any want of inclination on the part of the living race of English-men, but from the sheer impossibility of remedying in one year the accumulated evils of ages, and of elevating the character of a people too poor and sorrow stricken to attempt to elevate themselves ...

(*Illustrated London News* (25 November 1848))

In England, in the latter stages of the famine, the moralist fixation was attacked by the Irish correspondent of the Illustrated London News, *one of the few British newspapers to pursue a humanitarian line towards the end of the famine. It was argued that measures allegedly introduced to give 'justice' had merely increased suffering.*

... The present condition of the Irish ... has been mainly brought on by ignorant and vicious legislation. The destruction of the potato for one season, though a great calamity, would not have doomed them, fed as they were by the taxes of the state and charity of the world, to immediate decay; but a false theory, assuming the name of political economy, with which it has no more to do than the slaughter of the Hungarians by General Haynau, led the landlords and the legislature to believe that it was a favourable opportunity for changing the occupation of the land and the cultivation of the soil from potatoes to corn. When more food, more cultivation, more employment, were the requisites for maintenance of the Irish in existence, the legislature and the landlords set about introducing a species of cultivation that could only be successful by requiring fewer hands, and turning potato gardens, that nourished the maximum of human beings, into pasture grounds for bullocks, that nourished only the minority ...

The Poor Law, said to be for the relief of the people and the means of their salvation, was the instrument of their destruction. In their terrible distress, from that temporary calamity with which they were visited, they were to have no relief unless they gave up their holdings. That law, too, laid down a form for evicting the people, and gave the sanction and encouragement of legislation to exterminating them. Calmly and quietly, but very ignorantly – though we cheerfully exonerate all parties from any malevolence – they not only committed a great mistake, a terrible blunder, which in legislation is worse than a crime – but calmly and quietly from Westminster itself, which is the centre of civilization, did the decree go forth which has made the temporary but terrible visitation of a potato rot the means of exterminating, through the slow process of disease and houseless starvation, nearly half of the Irish ...

(Illustrated London News (15 December 1849))

During the period 1841–51, the population of Ireland fell from 8,175,124 – the highest recorded – to 6,552,385. The overall decline was 20 per cent, but in some counties it was higher. The population of County Mayo fell by 29 per cent, from 388,887 to 274,830, through death and emigration. Emigration became a long-term legacy of the Famine, with each successive census showing a decline in population, which reached a low of 109,525 in County Mayo in 1971. It could still be argued, however, that given demographic trends, birth and death rates and substantial pre-famine emigration, the population was likely to have begun to decrease, or at least stabilise, regardless of the famine.

Population of County Mayo 1841-1911

Year	Males	Females	Total	Percentage change
1841	194,198	194,689	388,887	
1851	133,264	141,235	274,499	−29.41
1861	125,636	129,160	254,796	−7.18
1871	120,877	125,153	246,030	−3.44
1881	119,421	125,791	245,212	−0.33
1891	107,498	111,536	219,034	−10.68
1901	97,564	101,602	199,166	−9.07
1911	96,345	95,832	192,177	−3.51

(W.E. Vaughan and A.J. Fitzpatrick (eds.), *Irish Historical Statistics: Population 1821–1971*

(Dublin, 1978), p. 14)

1841–1851! Those ten short years have seen more grievous and overwhelming changes in Ireland than befall to other countries in the course of centuries. Down the long files of figures on the census Table is indexed one of the most mournful histories the eye of GOD has ever rested upon. Within ten years the world has advanced greatly toward its goal – noble thoughts and actions keeping apt harmony with the music of the spheres ... But Ireland has struggled and starved for ten years ... Of all the wide world, ours is the only country we know of that, during this decade, has retrograded in the scale of national strength and liberty ...

(*The Nation*, 12 July, 1851)

Journalist, historian and Young Ireland activist John Mitchel (1815–75) was largely responsible for the dissemination of the idea of the 'Great Famine' in which Irish history was constructed from the arrival of Cromwell to the 1848 Rising as a catalogue of English oppression of Ireland and an indictment of colonial rule. In this interpretation, the famine was the result of a sinister intention on the part of Britain to rid Ireland of its surplus population. In the following work the religious context of the times was turned into a powerful political argument, the idea being encapsulated in Mitchel's most famous comment, that, 'The almighty indeed, sent the potato blight, but the English created the famine'. Mitchel's thesis had a particularly profound impact among Irish emigrants in North America, but also on future historians and in popular fiction.

... How an island which is said to be an integral part of the richest empire on the globe – and the most fertile part of that empire ... should in five years lose two and a half millions of its people (more than one fourth) by hunger, and fever the consequence of hunger, and flight beyond sea to escape from hunger, – while that empire of which it is said to be a part was all the while advancing in wealth, prosperity, and comfort, at a faster pace than ever before ... Rearing its accursed gables and pinnacles of Tudor Barbarism, and staring boldly with its detestable mullioned windows, as if to mock those wretches who still cling to liberty and mud cabins – seeming to them, in their perennial half-starvation, like a Temple erected to the fates, or like the fortress of Giant Despair, whereinto he draws them one by one, and devours them there: – the Poor-house ...

There began [in 1847] to be an eager desire in England to get rid of the Celts by *emigration*; for though they were perishing fast of hunger and typhus, they were not perishing fast enough. It was inculcated by the English press that the temperament and disposition of the Irish people fitted them peculiarly for some remote country in the East, or in the West, – in fact, for any country but their own; – that Providence had committed some mistake in causing them to be born in Ireland ... Mr Murray, a Scotch banker, writes a pamphlet upon the proper measures for Ireland. 'The surplus population of Ireland,' says Mr Murray, 'have been raised *precisely* for those pursuits, which the unoccupied regions of North America require.' Which might appear strange to anybody but a respectable banker; – a population expressly trained, and that *precisely*, to suit any country except their own ... the subjection of Ireland is now probably assured until some external shock should break up that monstrous commercial firm, the British Empire ... its cup of abomination is not yet running over ... so long as this hatred and horror shall last – so long as our nation refuses to become, like Scotland, a contented province of the enemy, Ireland is not finally subdued. The passionate aspiration for Irish nationhood will outlive the British Empire ... And lastly, I have shown you in the course of this narrative – that the depopulation of the country was not only encouraged by artificial means, namely the Outdoor Relief Act, the Labour Rate Act [which put the cost of relief works on the rates], and the emigration schemes, but that extreme care and diligence were used to prevent relief coming to the doomed island from abroad; and that the benevolent contributions of Americans and other foreigners were turned aside from their destined objects – not, let us say, in order that none should be saved alive, but that no interference should be made with the principles of political economy ...

(John Mitchel, *The Last Conquest of Ireland (Perhaps)* (Dublin, 1861))

Mortality in 1847 as a Percentage of 1841 Population in Certain Counties

County	Percentage
Armagh	3.3
Clare	3.6
Cork, East Riding	5.0
Cork, West Riding	3.3
Fermanagh	3.2
Galway	3.0
Kerry	3.1
Leitrim	3.9
Longford	3.0
Louth	3.1
Queen's County	3.0
Roscommon	3.1
Tipperary, North Riding	4.2
Tipperary, South Riding	4.1
Waterford	3.3

(S.H. Cousens, 'The Regional Variation in Mortality during the Great Irish Famine', in *Proceedings of the Royal Irish Academy* (lxiii), section C, no. 3 (1963))

The famine resulted in the consolidation of farm holdings. One farm in four disappeared between 1845 and 1851 and the decline was concentrated in the holdings of less than 15 acres. The average size of farms increased during the famine years; a product of famine deaths and evictions; but thereafter farm numbers and size changed little between 1851 and the First World War. The cottier or labourer class were most affected by the famine, and farmers in the post-famine period were loath to permit labourers to impinge on their holdings (grant conacre), in many instances a reaction to the rates bills of the famine years, when farmers were burdened with the upkeep of labourers. The disappearance of this more impoverished class had serious implications for the social structure of rural life, and indeed the values, attitudes and prosperity of those who had consolidated their land. There was also a huge turnover in the landlord class, and the Encumbered Estates Act of 1849 facilitated the speedy sale of bankrupt estates. By 1870 most Irish landlords were newcomers with smaller estates.

Number and Sizes of Holdings in 1847 and 1851

	1847	1851
1 acre or less	73,016	37,728
Above 1 acre and not exceeding 5 acres	139,041	88,083
Above 5 acres and not exceeding 15 acres	269,534	191,854
Above 15 acres and not exceeding 30 acres	164,337	141,311
Above 30 Acres	157,097	149,090
Total Holdings	**803,025**	**608,066**

Number and Sizes of Holdings in 1852, 1861 and 1871

	1852	1861	1871
Not exceeding 1 acre	35,058	41,561	48,448
Above 1, not exceeding 15	263,869	269,400	246,192
Above 15, not exceeding 50	209,215	213,700	211,434
Above 50, not exceeding 300	71,825	75,464	76,758
Above 200	9,504	9,919	9,758
Total Holdings	**589,471**	**610,044**	**592,590**

(Figures taken from the Annual Agricultural Returns. Cited in Liam Kennedy et al.
Mapping the Great Irish Famine, p. 163)

Some were not shy to recall their neighbours who profited from the famine. Here are the testaments of Thomas O'Flynn and John Melody, from Attymass, Ballina, County Mayo.

Some local families were unaffected by the famine or at least they managed to live. These mostly composed the agents of the landlords – bailiffs, bog-rangers, wood-rangers, game-keepers, hands, etc. Not only did they manage to live but they got large tracts of land adjoining their own, when holdings were forsaken by those who emigrated.

A local landlord has a farm of about 200 acres and practically half of this was in the possession of seasonal tenants before the famine. A good deal of this is small fields, some not bigger than the usual 'cabbage garden'.

Millers were supposed to be the best off during the period. They held a quarter of the grain they received for distribution to beggars. There were five grinding mills in the parish, four in one townland which has yet the reputation of being best off in '46, '47. The upper class had one ambition in those days, to marry the miller's daughter, as she had a good fortune.

(IFC 1069: 351–78, Cathal Póirtéir, *Famine Echoes*, p. 216)

LIST OF DOCUMENTS

List of Documents

FURTHER READING

Further Reading

Bourke, Austin, 'The Visitation of God?' *The Potato and the Great Irish Famine* (Dublin: Lilliput Press, 1993)

Boyce, George and O'Day, Alan (eds.), *The Making of Modern Irish History: Revisionism and the Revisionist Controversy* (London: Routledge, 1996)

Brady, Ciarán (ed.), *Interpreting Irish History: The Debate on Historical Revisionism 1938–1994* (Dublin: Irish Academic Press, 1994)

Crawford, Margaret (ed.), *The Hungry Stream: Essays on Emigration and Famine* (Belfast: Institute of Irish Studies, 1997)

Daly, Mary, *The Famine in Ireland* (Dundalk: Dundalgan Press, 1986)

Deane, Seamus, *Strange Country: Modernity and Nationhood in Irish Writing since 1790* (Oxford: Oxford University Press, 1997)

Dudley Edwards, Robert and William, Desmond (eds.), *The Great Famine: Studies in Irish History 1845–52* (Dublin: Lilliput Press, 1994)

Eagleton, Terry, *Heathcliff and the Great Hunger: Studies in Irish Culture* (London: Verso, 1996)

Fitzpatrick, David, *Oceans Of Consolation: Personal Accounts of Irish Migration to Australia* (Ithaca and London: Cork University Press, 1994)

Foster, Roy, *Modern Ireland 1600–1972* (Harmondsworth: Penguin, 1990)

Gray, Peter, *Famine, Land and Politics* (Dublin: Irish Academic Press, 1999)

Hayden, Tom (ed.), *Irish Hunger: Personal Reflections on the Legacy of the Famine* (Dublin: Wolfhound Press, 1997)

Kennedy, Liam; Ell, Paul; Crawford, E. M.; and Crawford, L. A. (eds.), *Mapping the Great Irish Famine* (Dublin: Four Courts Press, 1999)

Killen, John (ed.), *The Famine Decade: Contemporary Accounts, 1841–51* (Belfast: Blackstaff Press, 1995)

Kinealy, Christine, *This Great Calamity: The Irish Famine, 1845–52* (Dublin: Gill & Macmillan, 1994)

King, Carla (ed.), *Famine, Land and Culture in Ireland: A Documentary History* (Dublin: University College Dublin Press, 2000)

Kissane, Noel, *The Irish Famine: A Documentary History* (Dublin: National Library of Ireland, 1995)

Laxton, Edward, *The Famine Ships: The Irish Exodus to America 1846–51* (London: Bloomsbury, 1997)

Mokyr, Joel, *Why Ireland Starved: A Quantitative and Analytical History of the Irish Economy 1800–50* (London: Allen and Unwin, 1983)

Morash, Chris, *Writing the Irish Famine* (Oxford: Oxford University Press, 1995)

Morash, Chris and Hayes, Richard (eds.), *Fearful Realities: New Perspectives on the Famine* (Dublin: Irish Academic Press, 1996)

Neal, Frank, *Black '47: Britain and the Famine Irish* (London: Macmillan, 1997)

Nicholson, Asenath, *Annals of the Famine in Ireland* edited by Maureen Murphy (Dublin: Lilliput Press, 1998)

O'Gráda, Cormac, *Black '47 and Beyond: The Great Irish Famine in History, Economy and Memory* (Princeton: Princeton University Press, 1999)

O'Gráda, Cormac, *Ireland: A New Economic History 1780–1939* (Oxford: Oxford University Press, 1995)

O'Gráda, Cormac, *The Great Irish Famine* (Cambridge: Cambridge University Press, 1996)

Póirtéir, Cathal, *A Famine Echoes* (Dublin: Gill & Macmillan, 1995)

Póirtéir, Cathal (ed.), *The Great Irish Famine: The Thomas Davis Lectures* (Cork: Mercier Press, 1995)

Scally, Robert James, *The End of the Hidden Ireland: Rebellion, Famine and Emigration* (Oxford: Oxford University Press, 1996)

Vaughan, W.E., *Landlords and Tenants in Mid-Victorian Ireland* (Oxford: Oxford University Press, 1994)

INDEX

Index